SOCIAL EDUCATIO
AND SOCIAL UNDERSTA

WITHDRAWN

Social Education
and Social
Understanding

Edited by John Elliott and Richard Pring

UNIVERSITY OF LONDON PRESS LTD

57934

ISBN 0 340 16342 9 Boards
ISBN 0 340 16343 7 Unibook

University of London Press Ltd
St Paul's House, Warwick Lane, London EC4P 4AH

Text set in 11/12 pt. Monotype Bembo, printed
by letterpress, and bound in Great Britain at
The Pitman Press, Bath.

Contents

Introduction

The first two articles in this collection point out the increasing interest in social education. This interest is reflected in a proliferation of new courses bearing such titles as 'social education', 'social studies', 'personal relationships', 'integrated studies', 'community service', and 'the humanities', but in each case claims are made about 'social education' in some sense.

However, despite this common concern for social education, teachers do not (upon examination) seem to be talking about the same thing, to share the same assumptions or to have in mind the same practical problems —even where they employ the same language. The experience of some of the writers of these essays is that beneath a rather superficial agreement about the importance of social education there are radically different conceptions of what it means. Not that these different conceptions are easy to elicit. There is often a discrepancy between rationale offered as a description of the aims and principles of a course and the assumptions actually implicit in practice.

The six contributors to this collection have all taught in secondary schools, and some of them have witnessed or participated in the teaching of 'social education', All are aware of the difficulties of fostering communication between schools about work on social education and of making such work accessible to students in colleges and departments of education in a form which genuinely reflects practice and is open to critical examination. Hence these essays provide a background of ideas against which reflection on what is meant by social education, as it is practised in particular contexts, might profitably take place.

However, if the reader is hoping that out of these essays some unified, coherent, and internally consistent view of social education will emerge, he will be disappointed. Each contributor approaches the subject from the standpoint of rather different practical concerns. Hugh Sockett is concerned with the way teachers are being advised to plan social education courses; Richard Pring with changing the narrow, uncritical vision behind some courses devised for the less able; David Bridges with the importance of coming to understand social relations beyond our own society; Charles Bailey with the need for a *person*-based approach to social education; Peter Scrimshaw with the problem of relating the ordinary language of the pupil to the specialized languages of the social science disciplines; and John Elliott with the way controversial social situations and acts are handled by teachers in the classroom. Even this diversity cannot do justice to the full range of issues connected with planning a social education curriculum.

Nonetheless, although each contribution focuses on different problems, the approach to these problems is similar. All believe in the importance of philosophical reflection as a background against which central problems in social education need to be clarified and tackled. Moreover, the contributors share the common belief that education is about intellectual development and that more can be done in this respect with 'the average and below-average child' than is popularly assumed. Hence, the essays retain a unity of approach and educational standpoint, despite differences in detail. Arguments are interrelated. What is said in one essay is illustrated in greater detail in another. This is not simply a collection of independent essays; the essays are interdependent and complement one another in their general agreement on what the difficulties are, on matters of approach and on what education is about.

Complex Notion of Social Education

Social education means many different things to many different people. In the first article Richard Pring indicates the growing popularity of social education in current literature, particularly in government reports and in Schools Council working papers and projects (see the Appendix for a list of these). But this is by no means a peculiarly British phenomenon. Hugh Sockett, in the following contribution, points out how certain views of social education are deeply rooted in an American tradition and an American literature. Indeed possibly, as Pring later argues, the educationally most powerful and fruitful notion of social education is to be found in the work of Dewey and Kilpatrick, who saw education as the most powerful force for social reconstruction.

Nevertheless, it is important to distinguish between different conceptions or different aims, which fall beneath the title social education. These may be as narrow as certain specific skills and pieces of information, or as broad as moral education itself; they may be concerned with developing certain attitudes deemed to be socially useful or with making (under the guise of socialization) some logical point about the social nature of education itself; they may aim to foster active change within society or simply to understand certain aspects of it.

The range of possible meanings needs to be made explicit, and Pring distinguishes some of these. Particular ones are taken up in subsequent articles. For example, Charles Bailey looks in greater detail at those aspects of social education which are very close to moral education; John Elliott examines the particular concern of social education for the world of work, criticizing the identification of this with superficial information about careers; David Bridges (in his first contribution) analyses another specific aim, that of understanding society, but warns against the common inter-pretation of this as mere description of society. Each in turn, while picking out different aspects of social education, shares the common assumption about education, that is about the development of knowledge and under-standing, and that these must respect the peculiar nature of the subject matter they are concerned with (namely social meaning). Knowledge and understanding cannot be reduced either to prespecified skills, or to pieces of information.

Social Understanding

At the centre of social *education* (as apposed to training) there will be not simply the acquisition of skills or the gleaning of certain information, but the development of understanding—understanding of social pheno-mena, of society, of human relationships, and possibly, of social meanings. However, there is a difficulty. How can this sort of understanding be characterized? What sort of understanding is peculiar to social phenomena? Can this understanding be differentiated from other sorts of understanding? Are there, for instance, concepts, principles, procedures and skills, which need to be mastered by the pupil if he is to acquire social understanding? Can social studies be a discipline in the same way that physics, biology, and mathematics are disciplines? And what are the true conditions peculiar to judgements in this area?

It is in this connection that David Bridges' first contribution to this volume is of particular interest. He points to certain difficulties of a logical kind inherent in understanding other societies. Unlike the natural scientist, the student of other societies and other social groups cannot remain an outsider, an external observer. Social phenomena are not like natural phenomena. Their understanding requires a grasp of events as the partici-pant sees them—by way of the rules and concepts and organizing principles which *they* employ. Indeed a criticism of some sociology (and thus of the social studies which use this sociology) is that it adopts the techniques of the natural scientists and observes 'from the outside'.

Charles Bailey tackles a similar problem from a slightly different angle. What is the special kind of knowledge and understanding that one is concerned with in social development? Frequently it is summed up in such words as 'empathy' and 'sympathy'. Thus we might be told that, in social education, we seek to develop empathic knowledge of others, a sympathetic concern for others' problems or some insight into how others feel. Bailey, in a close analysis of these terms, distinguishes between their different uses and concludes that, despite their popular appeal, they do not assist our analysis of social understanding. Rather is the peculiarity of social understanding dependent upon the conceptional framework employed or the basic categories that structure our thinking in this area. For instance, to talk about 'persons'—to have understood this concept—is to enter into a whole area of discourse with its connected concepts, its related values, its peculiar modes of argument. And this is where social and moral education overlap. For central to moral education is awareness of, and respect for, people as persons.

Nonetheless there are still some features peculiar to social understanding which need to be explored further and which have important implications for teaching. If, as David Bridges argues, to understand a social relationship or a social organization is to see it as the participants see it, then there may be different understandings of what externally seems to be the same event or happening. Thus an important element in social education may be to explore reflectively rather than argumentatively the different points of view on some social issue. It is this aspect of social understanding which John Elliott examines. From a philosophical position (developed in greater detail elsewhere) concerning the nature of understanding social issues where there are divergent views, he draws out the implications for teaching strategies in the area of 'people and work'. The same problems, the same arguments, and the same consequent strategies are, of course, relevant to a range of issues on which society tolerates different positions. Indeed, in the rather loose conception of social education that prevails, Elliott could have dealt with other controversial issues such as 'poverty', 'relations between the sexes', 'violence', 'war', etc. However, the interesting twist which lies in this particular choice is that it is the world of work which is so frequently central to social studies courses but in a form that is constricting and uninspiring. That it is an area of *educational* potential, for deep exploration and understanding, is frequently neglected in favour of a catalogue of rather boring facts and uninspiring advice.

The Language of Social Studies

The constant theme of this collection of essays is the peculiar nature of social understanding and thus of social education. Hence, there is the need to examine more explicitly the language used for judgements about society and about social phenomena. Peter Scrimshaw tackles this in some depth. The educational implications of his analysis are not so immediate. But it is apparent from the other contributions that central to the more obvious educational questions are these peculiarly philosophical ones about the nature of language. Scrimshaw therefore is dealing explicitly with some of the issues which are implicitly revealed by the others.

It is interesting that within sociology itself, and in particular within sociology of education, sociological accounts of society have come under radical attack. Thus we are told that there is a need to distinguish between the data of the natural sciences and the data of the social sciences. The latter are 'social meanings' and are constructed by the participating members of the social group. They are not fixed data, but are constantly changing as the 're-negotiation of meanings' between people takes place. For too long, the argument goes, sociology has taken over accepted common-sense explanations of social experience and treated these as 'unproblematic'. However, the process of achieving these common-sense understandings does itself need to be examined and questioned, and the common-sense meanings treated as problematic.

It is not for this book to arbitrate in the soul-searching of sociologists, but it is interesting to note how at the centre of the sociological account and understanding of society is a concern for the status of the language employed and of the judgements made within the conceptional framework of commonsense. Peter Scrimshaw is right therefore to direct attention in a book on social education to the nature of the language employed in talking about social experience and its connection with common-sense understanding of other persons and other societies.

A variation on this sociological questioning of the data of social theory is the view that the validity of particular knowledge claims is relatie to socio-historical conditions. Thus what constitutes knowledge is deter-mined (or 'legitimized') by those who are in control of its growth, dissem-ination, and transmission. This, of course, takes us beyond the present concern, but it does shed light upon what is meant by the social nature of knowledge and understanding. That there is a connection between objectivity and inter-personal agreement is true. But it is fallacious to argue from that to the relativity of knowledge and to its contingency upon social control. Richard Pring indicates the general line of argument here, the points that should be questioned, and the educational implications.

The Curriculum

The general line of argument pursued in the majority of these essays has implications for the way one sets about designing a social education curri-culum. In giving knowledge and understanding a position of central importance they come out against a view of social education which is content to concentrate on 'doing' divorced from reflection. Hugh Sockett argues that a social education based on the development of cognitive abilities cannot be designed according to the 'behavioural objectives model' of curriculum planning. As an example of this model he cites the attempt of Professor P. H. Taylor to analyse the aims of social education into a set of pre-specified behavioural skills which constitute the realization of these aims. Sockett argues that social abilities like competence, confidence and cooperation are necessarily related to an agent's understanding of his duties and rights in a social situation and cannot be reduced to a list of physical skills. He suggests that 'the behavioural objectives model' of curriculum design is only applicable in those areas where instruction is particularly appropriate, that is, in the area of physical skills. Not all teaching need be of the instructional kind and it is in the false assumption that teaching can be reduced to instruction and therefore to the intention to bring about certain pre-specified behaviours that the curriculum planner often makes a serious mistake.

Hugh Sockett then goes on to suggest that statements of curriculum aims, rather than being general descriptions of learning outcomes (behavioural or otherwise), are guides to the teachers' decision-making. This relates to Richard Pring's analysis of the concept of aim. Aims refer not so much to some states of affairs which are contingently related to the activities through which they are pursued, but rather they describe the nature or point of the activity itself. As an example, Pring refers to the doctor's aim of 'curing the sick'. This is not a description of a state of affairs which the doctor's activities result in, but a description of the activities themselves. It defines how the doctor sees what he is doing and provides him with criteria for selecting his objectives *qua* doctor. However, from 'curing the sick' one cannot deduce what a doctor's precise objectives ought to be at any given moment. He may cure the sick by preventing a patient from dying of pneumonia or from suffering from a rash. But one cannot pre-specify in advance of a situation exactly what objectives the doctor ought to have in mind. Similarly one cannot pre-specify in advance of particular educational situations what precise cognitive abilities students need to acquire. The aims of a social studies curriculum provide a general description of a teacher's activities in a particular area which guides his selection of objectives and curriculum activities but does not stifle the need for sensitive judgement in particular circumstances. The attempt to translate aims into specific objectives is misguided since it negates the whole function of aims, which is to guide judgement in complex situations without circumscribing it too narrowly. Hence Sockett's remark that the so-called 'rational' activity of planning by pre-specified objectives, if seriously attempted by teachers, 'would be, to put it mildly, irrational'.

John Elliott's description of the design of the Humanities Project puts some 'flesh' on these arguments. The Project is well known for its opposition to pre-specification of teaching objectives as a basis for curriculum design. Elliott describes how from a statement of aim the project derived a specification of a teaching method in the form of principles of procedure, to guide the teacher's conduct in the classroom. This type of design has been described by the project's director, Lawrence Stenhouse, as the 'in-put model'. Instead of specifying a curriculum in terms of output, or terminal learnings, it is specified in terms of teaching principles (in-put) which are implied by the aims of teaching in a particular area.

David Bridges, in his final contribution, raises questions about an area of growing interest—international understanding. It pulls together many of the points made in previous contributions, in particular: the problems inherent in understanding others and other societies; the problems in determining curriculum content and purposes; the problems concerning teaching divisive and controversial subject matter.

I

Socialization as an Aim of Education

RICHARD PRING

SECTION I
Current Concern for Social Studies

This essay examines what socialization, as an aim of education, could mean. There are two reasons why this is necessary. First, it is a fact that some people think education is concerned with socializing children, preparing them for citizenship, initiating them into a democratic way of life and so on. *The Times Educational Supplement* constantly advertises posts for social studies departments, civics departments, even social relationship departments. The Plowden Report sees one obvious purpose of primary education as fitting children for the society into which they will grow up. Schools Council projects have been established to see how this can be done, and the Council's working papers suggest all sorts of approaches. Socialization therefore, is one form or another, is an 'in' thing to be doing. What then is the teacher, who is committed to socializing his pupils, aiming at? What would count as having taught successfully in this matter? How would one recognize socialized children if one met them?

A second, less practical reason for sorting out what this means is that those who wish to socialize seem of the opinion that they have grasped some logical truth about education, that socialization says something about education and it is not simply a useful end towards which education might be directed. But, as in the case of those who talk about children growing or realizing their potential or being stimulated, it is all a bit woolly and the objectives are hazy. It is always a useful task to worry away at hazy notions like this until they are clear enough to be seen for what they are worth.

The Crowther Report (1959, chapter 17) advocated compulsory attendance at county colleges on one day a week for those who left school at fifteen because, for one thing, further education would help the students to mature into 'profitable citizens'. 'Profitable citizens' could mean many things, but Crowther indicates that profitable citizens would be those who *first* find their way successfully about the adult world (e.g. spending their money sensibly) and who *secondly* have defined a standard of moral values to guide them through the wide variety of choices confronting them.

The difficulties here are apparent. What counts as success in one's journeying around the adult world and what counts as having *defined* a standard of moral values (let alone whether or not they are correct moral values) is not at all clear. But for the moment we can rest with the conclusion that two aspects of educating for citizenship have been distinguished: (1) learning about the adult world and (2) sorting out one's moral standards. And that's a start.

When one turns to the Newsom Report the process of socializing begins to warm up. After all, one is now concerned with the lower half of our future. The trouble with the lower half of our future is that they aren't really able to follow the rather academic curriculum that has been the lot of most children in secondary schools, and, they are not really up to pursuing knowledge for its own sake. Knowledge has to be 'relevant' and 'practical'. Relevant to what? Practical for what? Relevant, says Newsom, to adult life. They won't become mathematicians and scientists and historians, but they will become husbands and wives and mums and dads. So at least let us prepare them or educate them for that. 'Their full vocation is' to quote the report 'to grow up as people who can take their place in the world with some degree of proper pride in what they do . . .' (Newsom Report, 1963, chapter 5). They must learn to manage complex human relations and they need guidance on social manners in every sense.

'Relevance to adult life' is like a theme running through Newsom and it is this phrase which gives the clue to such variations as 'vocational', 'practical', 'realistic'. But how are we to understand 'relevance to adult life'? One very good way to the understanding of any statement of aims is to look at the examples.

Newsom gives an example of preparation for adult life from a girls' school in the Midlands industrial area, with many social problems. The aims are:

1 To give the girls opportunities to be socially acceptable, and to behave socially in a way which, in any community, usually falls to the most able;
2 To link their work with their future hope—marriage. The home, the family, the baby, the growing children, are subjects of study. Mothercraft etc.;
3 To link their school work with life outside, and to provide experience out of school with their school work.

This is a particularly important example because it helps to fill out the notion of being prepared for adult life, and it is this notion which has given momentum to so much current development within our secondary schools. There is more than a suspicion that what one is offering is a limited diet of social training, acquisition of the values and skills which prevail in that society, anticipation of the situations which the child will soon meet in his or her milieu, competence to deal with practical difficulties when they arise. I think that it is this limitation of vision, this narrowing of horizons that provoked the following letter from a headmaster in *The Times Educational Supplement* shortly after the publication of the Newsom Report:

> If we can teach him chastity he will not need to know anything about engagement and marriage at the age of 15. But if we fail to teach him about Nelson, then no matter how full his head may be stuffed with family planning and the welfare state and pensions I still say he will not be a good citizen of this country.

The Newsom Report therefore gave a momentum to the growing belief that the school should be concerned with specifically social aims of education, a belief reinforced by the prospect of an extra year at school.

The Schools Council produced several pamphlets which indicated the direction in which things were moving. Working Paper No. 2, Raising the School Leaving Age' says that the curriculum should be holistic . . . it should possess organic unity, and the organizing principle most likely to provide a sound basis for development is the study of Man, and of human society, its needs and purposes'. The publication 'Another Year—to endure or enjoy?' by the Schools Council Welsh Committee gives its own examples of programmes that are 'relevant' or 'real' for those compelled to stay on another year. Such programmes are variously called 'social training', 'learning for living', 'work experience', 'social education' (the aim of which, by the way, is the 'right approach to life'). The most famous of all these publications is, however, Schools Council Working Paper No. 11, 'Society and the Young School Leaver' which, in examining attempts in schools to provide meaningful courses for the Newsom child, gave examples of successful courses. Such courses helped the pupil to understand society and were, by and large, connected with the world of work. Syllabuses, illustrated and recommended, were 'The Family', 'Work Experience', 'Familiarity with the Adult World', 'Myself and the World', 'Public Utilities', 'Water Supply', and 'The 97 Bus route'. In these courses pupils would be addressed by members of the local community; and they would visit magistrates' courts, day nurseries, and the town hall. In Schools Council Working Paper No. 17 'Community Service and the Curriculum', the *educational* value of helping old people, assisting with meals-on-wheels, visiting the sick and so on is recommended.

Subsequently semi-official endorsement is given to work for organizations such as Task Force in many schools—sometimes as part of the curriculum.

We have therefore a lively and quite new set of activities in many schools which is vaguely called social education. From the brief survey I have given of these activities one can say that they comprise these following quite different aims or objectives:

1 To learn about the local society (e.g. where the town hall is, where you will one day draw your pension and so on).
2 To understand how society works (basic sociology and economics as distinct academic subjects).
3 To learn to be responsible (which in no way seems different from what is ordinarily meant by moral education).
4 To have the right social attitudes (which could mean touching your forelock to the squire or demonstrating for a better world—depending on the views of the teacher).

Social studies courses seem to aim at one if not more than one of the above objectives. And it is because of this that they are subject to different sorts of criticism. Briefly and rather dogmatically I wish to indicate the different grounds for criticism.

SECTION 2
Critical Examination of these Aims

First, the sort of social studies programmes referred to in Working Paper No. 11 has been criticized by John White (1967). The gist of his argument is that by focusing the attention of the pupil upon the limited environment of his locality one is failing to educate. For education would seem to imply at least developing the capacity to look critically at values and beliefs, to weigh evidence and acquire standards of comparison and power of discrimination. But so long as one's knowledge is limited to the familiar and the immediate, one will not arrive at standards of comparison or at the critical questioning which is a mark of the educated man. White calls this 'Education in Obedience', that is, getting people to accept their lot. To learn how to vote may be a useful social training, but this does not make it a social education. It is this narrowness of vision or of perspective, this limiting of what is studied to the local and the immediate, which Bruner criticizes, and, in criticizing, has developed a social education project that incorporates the study of quite different forms of life and quite different cultures (see below p. 21 and Bruner, 1966, p. 73).

Social training, in the narrow and descriptive sense, must be distinguished from the social education envisaged by the social scientists. The sociologist would deplore the confusion of social studies, such as are proposed in Working Paper No. 11, with sociology. And yet this confusion is only too apparent in most of the recent literature. One must distinguish between, on the one hand, a descriptive account of the more obvious institutions in one's neighbourhood together with the rules and skills required to find one's way around these institutions and, on the other hand, the fundamental sociological concepts required for an understanding of those institutions and the way in which they affect the life of the individual. From the social scientist's point of view what is meant, at least in part, by socialization is the increased perspective, the increased understanding that arises from the disciplined study of a particular body of knowledge. This is more a claim for the addition of sociology to the syllabus than for an integration of the curriculum around such themes as 'Family', 'Work', and so on. That this distinction is recognized by some proposals for social studies is apparent from the more recent Schools Council work, in particular Working Paper No. 39.

If this is what is meant by social education, however, one must beware of two possible lines of development. The first is the false step from seeing social education as a scientific discipline in its own right to seeing social education as the core subject in an integrated curriculum, the focal point which determines what parts of history, geography, literature, religious knowledge, etc. are to be considered relevant. On these grounds it is necessary to criticize programmes of socialization such as are recommended by Vincent Rogers (1968). Rogers sees social studies as a discipline whose subject matter is 'the study of man both as an individual and as a member of a host of groups; with man both changing and adjusting to his environment'. But here we have a confusion which it is most important to recognize because it is at the centre of many social studies programmes. Such themes as 'man and his environment' are essentially of an inter-disciplinary nature. It is difficult to see what discipline or what study would not count as a contribution to such a broad organizing concept. The social scientist has no special claims here—no more so than the poet, the historian, the theologian, the geographer. That integration of these elements is important is undeniable, but that social studies as a discipline (characterized therefore by its own peculiar concepts, its own mode of verification, its own logical procedures) should be the essential link in such an integration is something which has still to be argued for. I doubt very much that historians, geographers, theologians and poets would be pleased to see themselves as sub-species of sociology.

So far I have suggested that one should beware of two quite different objectives that might lurk beneath the aim of socializing children. The first is the limited and limiting vision that this might signify—training in the skills required to find one's way around one's own provincial environment. The second is a take-over bid by sociology made whilst defending itself as a discipline. It cannot be both a distinctive discipline and an integrating link in the curriculum. In other words, sociologists are welcome as experts in sociology, not as experts in the broader issues of man and society.

The third criticism of the objectives of social studies is of the failure very often to distinguish between factual and moral judgements. It is one thing to describe society and explain why things happen as they do; it is quite another to say what ought to happen. It is one thing to state what the values of a society are and how they originate; it is quite another to say what *is* valuable and to justify one's evaluation. Social studies as a discipline and as a science is concerned with description and explanation of norms and values; it cannot be concerned with prescription. This distinction is an important one. Hume pointed out that you cannot derive an 'ought' from an 'is'—statements about what you ought to do from statements setting out the facts. This logical hiatus between description and prescription is, of course, questionable. Nevertheless, the distinction must remain where one is attempting to distinguish *scientific* propositions from non-scientific ones. The *social sciences* cannot give us the answers to such questions as 'What should the children value in life?' or 'What is the right attitude to teach?'.

Social studies, on the other hand, whilst trading upon the objectivity which is claimed to characterize the disciplined examination of society, sneaks in this prescriptive element under the guise of socialization. It is as though social studies is concerned not just with the development of understanding, but with the inculcation of certain attitudes, specific values or norms, reactions and ways of behaving. And this prescriptive element, this socializing of the young into the ways of behaving and feeling of the older generation, is seen as a central function of education in general, and thereby of social studies in particular. According to Durkheim (1956), 'Education is the influence exercised by adult generations on those that are not yet ready for social life. Its object is to arouse and to develop in the child a certain number of physical, intellectual, and moral states which are demanded of him by both the political society as a whole and the special milieu for which he is specifically destined'. There is a certain view of sociology (and of education as an area of sociological examination) which sees schooling as essentially a socializing process, and the outcome of schooling to be an inculcation of those attitudes and norms which promote the preservation of that society. Education itself, and the different ways it develops, are a function of more far-reaching social forces or characteristics.

Education is essentially conservative. It is a training for adaptation, adjustment, fitting in. But is this education? And if not, need socialization have this meaning?

'Socialization' is a suspect word to many because it seems to imply not only knowledge and understanding of society by those who are socialized but also acceptance of the values and norms of that society. Thus the Newsom Report and the various working papers referred to seem as much concerned with the attitudes and values of the pupils as with the knowledge which they acquire. To train for citizenship seems to mean that one should inculcate certain values—respect for property, due deference to authority, the duty to vote, obedience to the law, loyalty to one's country. These would be the sort of features that distinguish the good citizen. Therefore, these would be the qualities that we must teach our pupils if they are to be properly socialized. They must learn the proper rules of behaviour.

It is not difficult therefore to pinpoint the difficulties that underlie our suspicions of socialization. What rules of conduct is one to teach? Who is the moral expert? How does one qualify to pronounce on matters of right and wrong? Given that the public no longer accepts a licence in moral theology as such a qualification, would it be any wiser to accept a degree in sociology? If not, then to whom should one go for one's moral education? These difficulties are central to an understanding of socialization in so far as socialization is concerned (in the words of Newsom) with developing a sense of responsibility and the right social attitudes. How can one teach the right social attitudes without indoctrinating or conditioning?

The most valuable social studies curriculum projects are the 'Humanities Curriculum Project' and 'Man: a Course of Study'. John Elliott, later in this book, examines in greater detail the principles and practice of the Humanities Curriculum Project in one area of social studies. It meets the criticisms I have mentioned, which could be levelled against so much work in this area, because it sees the need (a) to prepare young people for participation in social life (citizenship and all that) (b) to incorporate into this preparation some form of moral education, and (c) to distinguish this moral education from teaching a particular morality. The aim of the project is to provide materials upon which the pupils might base their enquiry into problems about which decisions have to be made. It is not the teacher who is to decide what should be done. The role of the teacher is that of providing evidence on which decision might be made and, in the *procedural* role of strict neutrality, providing the framework in which this evidence might be sifted and conclusions drawn. The Project, then, has made some sense of the Newsom proposals that schools should be concerned with the social education of pupils, for it has recognized the moral implications of such proposals without at the same time confusing them with the teaching of a particular set of moral values or rules.

MACOS (or 'Man: a Course of Study'), on the other hand, starts with three questions: what is human about human beings? How did they get that way? How can they be made more so? This initially looks like the sort of inter-disciplinary study, criticized earlier, which is the subject-matter of all subjects and not of a limited discipline. But Bruner in seeing it to be a course in social studies examines these questions from a particular perspective, and draws for intellectual content upon the disciplines within the social sciences—anthropology in particular. With the use of carefully selected evidence, crucial elements in social understanding are put across— such notions as 'culture', 'social structure', 'social function', 'role', 'inter-action'. MACOS, in other words, uses the tools, the evidence and the insights of developed social sciences to teach an understanding of basic concepts and principles.

SECTION 3
Socialization as an Intrinsic Aim of Education

It is crucial in defining socialization as an aim of education to make the distinction between aim or intention on the one hand and purposes or functions on the other. To talk of the aims of an activity is to clarify what that activity is. The aim is part of the meaning of the activity. One only knows that a person is teaching or running a race or preaching in so far as one is aware of his aim or intention. To talk therefore of socialization as an aim of education would, if aim was being used in this sense, be to characterize the sort of activity which we wish to evaluate as educational. Socialization would be filling out our meaning of the word education. It would be saying that for any activity to count as education it would have to be characterized by aims which were social in character.

This distinction is crucial. It might be illustrated by the ambiguity of 'aim' where one says 'The aim of being a doctor is to cure the sick' and 'The aim of being a doctor is to make money'. The first proposition is necessarily true; the second proposition only contingently so. In the first case, 'curing the sick' *must* characterize the intentions of those whose activities are described as 'doctoring'. This is to be contrasted with the interpretation of aim as the function of, or the reason for, education— where socialization is not seen as an explication of the meaning of the concept education but as a use to which education might or might not be put.

So many of the social studies programmes, and so many of the recommendations of the Newsom Report and its followers, can be read in the second sense—as a function or extrinsic purpose of education, not as necessarily characterizing all educational aims. Social studies might be seen as an addition to an existing programme; or citizenship might be seen as a particular function of an education which is defined and characterized quite independently. 'Citizenship' or 'maturity' or 'social relationships' might be seen as extrinsic aims—particular objectives which might be taken into account or might affect to some extent the conduct of the curriculum, but which are only contingently connected with the whole educational enterprise. It is when socialization is seen in this latter sense—as a set of objectives which serve as a reason for or a function of education— that the difficulties and criticisms that I raised are justified.

In what sense therefore can social socialization be regarded as an essential *characterization of* education as opposed to *a reason for* education? It is a common theme in educational theory that at least one thing can be said of education, namely, that it is concerned with the development of meaning, with getting people inside a particular form of thought. But the meaning of what we say and indeed of what we think depends upon the significance of the words we utter (and of symbols through which our thoughts are articulated) *within a language*. For it is within a language that the words and symbols are made intelligible. The meaning of a word depends upon the use to which it is put within a particular language. Languages have built in to them the meanings of words, the grammatical rules for establishing truth claims in the form of propositions, the logical rules of proceeding from premise to conclusion—meanings and rules that have been evolved and achieved through thousands of years of social life. It is not possible to think symbolically in total isolation from one's fellow beings. Thinking is essentially a social process, firstly, in so far as it is a symbolic activity and symbolism makes sense only in a social or communicative context; and secondly, because the truth claims that conclude thinking must be publicly testable. If a scientist makes certain claims for an experiment which are refuted by a fellow scientist, it would not be sufficient to say that his discoveries had been true for *him*. For as a scientist he has entered into a public activity, a social context, in which he thinks through a common language and in which his claims are verifiable by reference to public criteria. The same might be said of historians, mathematicians, philosophers, and so on. One feature therefore of education is its essentially public or social character and thus the aim of education (or at least the goals that one would normally characterize as educational) is to socialize people in the sense of initiating them into an essentially social activity.

The significance of socialization as pointing out the essentially social character of education has been a powerful force in a certain tradition of American education. For instance the stress on education for democracy was understood to mean more than a matter of teaching certain things as a means to achieving a certain political framework. Smith, Stanley and Shores (1957) argue that the determining factor in curriculum reconstruction should be the social aim of developing in each young American the democratic ideal and the democratic way of life. This should be the key to curriculum development and curriculum integration. That the democratic ideal as the aim of education can be open to criticism, even ridicule, cannot be doubted. Often in practice it trivializes education or is little better than indoctrination. At its best, however, it is a further attempt to explicate the very meaning of education. Democracy for Dewey, for instance, was not simply a system of government; it was a way of life which recognized how each member of society developed his beliefs and his values through participation in social life, how at the same time the social life itself developed through the critical appraisal and reflection of the individual, and how divisions within society or an authoritarian organization of society prevented the free exchange of ideas and criticism, thus stunting the growth of understanding and of knowledge. Democracy was for Dewey an aim of education, and as much as any experience that could claim to be educational, was open to criticism, questioning, fresh perspectives, and further development. Democracy was the recognition that the social consciousness evolved from the critical sharing of ideas by individuals and that the individual consciousness arose from participation in this social life. The greater, therefore, this interaction between each individual and the social environment in which he found himself, and the freer the interchange of ideas, the more evolved would be the social consciousness in which each individual participates. Education lay in the active participation in this social life. (See Dewey, 1916, in particular chapter 7.)

When Dewey and Kilpatrick in the 1930s, at the time of the depression, talked about education aiming at social reconstruction, they did not see education as a tool or as a means for achieving a particular sort of society. They saw rather that a reconstruction of the educational system and curriculum, which recognized the essentially social nature of knowledge and thought, would lead to a society based on shared ideals and beliefs, and on a respectful tolerance of the ideas of each individual. Each individual plays a part, no matter how insignificant, in the formation of the social framework of values, beliefs and understandings. (See Kilpatrick, 1933.)

SECTION 4
Misunderstandings in the Sociology of Knowledge

On the other hand there are dangers in basing an educational system on a recognition of the social nature of knowledge. These dangers are exemplified in the recent attempts by sociologists to account for the structure of knowledge, and thereby for the organization of the curriculum in so far as this reflects the structure of knowledge. There is a tradition in the sociology of knowledge, rooted in Hegel and Marx but also manifest more recently in Mannheim, according to which all knowledge is socially conditioned. Thus, according to Marx, any construction of a body of knowledge is inextricably linked to the interests of those who produce it. It follows that any critical examination of a body of knowledge is, in effect, a critical examination of those who produce it. Whatever the arguments (no matter how forceful or valid they seem) they are explicable in terms of the ideological framework within which they have been developed.

This on the surface must appear at least plausible, if what I said previously about the social nature of knowledge is true. A language is a public thing, and by being initiated into a particular language one is being initiated into a particular way of perception and evaluation. This is to some extent empirically borne out by social psychologists. It would seem a small step then to say that reality is socially constructed, and that any social construction is explicable in terms of the ideological framework of the producer of that knowledge. This would appear to inject a strong dose of relativism in to the value of one's educational objectives, and to undermine one's faith in the development of reason as something to be contradistinguished from mere prejudice.

The apparently small step, however, is in fact a veritable leap, but those who have contributed to the latest sociological account of knowledge seem not to be aware of it. I wish briefly to explain how this sociological account goes and then to indicate where it is fundamentally mistaken. This, I think, will explain more clearly firstly what I mean by saying that language, and thereby thinking through language, is essentially a socially developed capacity, and secondly, the limitations of such a statement. This in turn will help to clarify both the meaning and the limitations of identifying socialization with education.

In *Knowledge and Control*, (Young, 1971), a group of sociologists seem to be putting forward the following thesis about the sociology of knowledge.

Stage 1 Previously the sociology of education was concerned with the input and the output of something called the educational process, but the educational process itself was regarded as something given—a factor that went unanalysed. This, however, was mistaken, and it is the current task of sociology to explain the educational process itself— the actual management of knowledge.

Stage 2 The actual organization of knowledge is institutionalized and is explicable in terms of social origins. Any given body of knowledge is 'legitimized' by the current group in power. Change the power structure and you change the organization of knowledge. In effect 'all knowledge is shrouded in ideology'.

Stage 3 The present organization of knowledge, as reflected in the curriculum, is dominated by what are called the legitimizing categories of 'the scientific' and 'the rational'. It is further divided into particular rational organizations with their own particular conceptual structurings and principles of verification, the validity of which depends upon the degree of legitimization from those in power (for example, in the universities).

Stage 4 It is the job of sociology therefore to treat as problematic rather than absolute or necessary both the dominant categories of 'the scientific' and 'the rational' and the particular organizations of knowledge in the subjects and disciplines; and, in treating these as problematic, it is the job of sociology to enquire into and to explain them empirically, i.e. to relate them to particular social and power structures.

There seems to me to be a logical flaw in the reasoning. It is as follows: if 'the rational' is to be treated as a constructed reality, and if rationality is to be treated as problematic and in that sense open to enquiry, then either this treatment and this enquiry are themselves rational or they are irrational. If they are rational, then they presuppose the truth of that which they are questioning. If they are irrational, then there is no point in taking note of what they say. (This argument, of course, is as old as Aristotle—but it remains useful despite the apparent change in legitimizing authorities.) In other words there seem to be logical limits to empirical enquiry. Part of the process of understanding the structure of knowledge (and the language through which those knowledge claims are made) is to recognize the elements which are necessarily presupposed in the use of that language, in such a way that it is inconceivable that one should consider alternatives. But such an understanding (making explicit what is necessarily presupposed) is an epistemological rather than an empirical exercise. The extent of the sociologists' claims, therefore, seem to stem from a failure to distinguish between two quite different sorts of enquiry—a philosophical enquiry on the one hand about the necessary presuppositions of thinking in general and an empirical enquiry about particular ways of thinking. Failure to make this distinction seems to put them in an odd position. For if it is true, as Marx said, that producers of knowledge were actors constructing their own worlds according to the values of their own social background, one might rightly ask whether Marx saw himself as an actor, and, if not, why not. Put in another way, if (to quote C. Wright Mills) 'the rules of logic, whether practical or academic, are conventional, and will be shaped and selected in accordance with the purpose of the discourse or the intentions of the enquiries', one might well ask what is the status of this proposition or indeed of any part of the sociological enquiry into the *conventional* nature of the logical and conceptual categories through which we think and make knowledge claims.

My criticism of the recent excursion by sociologists into the organization of knowledge is valuable for my purposes because it brings out the limitations of (and thereby clarifies) my original statement that language and thought are socially developed and that consequently education is necessarily a socializing process to the extent that it is an introduction into a public language, a public world of meaning, through which we come to share a way of identifying, conceptualizing, and evaluating things in the world. But this public world of meaning is not open to any sort of development. There are logical limits. There is, at a basic level, a logical structuring to our thinking which is presupposed in any enquiry. There are implicit criteria of validity and of logical correctness, and a conceptual structuring which is so basic to our language that it cannot be treated as problematic and, in that sense, open to empirical enquiry and explanation. To learn to speak is to learn the valid ways of proceeding. And if it should be pointed out that what is regarded as valid or logically correct has in some areas of thought emerged relatively late, I would answer that such *empirical* findings have nothing to do with the *logical* status of that which has emerged—just as the temporary development of a child's *form* of thinking in no way affects the logical acceptability of the later stages of development.

Within the basic categorical structure of thought, however, there is scope for a wide range of differences about how precisely to classify and evaluate the experiences that we have. The sociologists do us a service to point this out again—if, indeed, it needed pointing out. But even here it is important to ask at what level is it open to anyone to restructure or to recreate the world in which he lives. Within the categorical framework that cannot be questioned (because it is presupposed in the very questioning), we have inherited a particular way of conceiving and of evaluating things. Although one should be aware of the social or ideological framework through which we come to accept certain beliefs, nonetheless there are limits to which we can question a large part of the system (even, if in theory that large part is not logically necessary) for we need at least one foot on the ground. The process of questioning takes place bit by bit, and requires prior initiation into the publicly developed and structured world which is being questioned.

In brief, education is socialization in the sense that it introduces people to a world of publicly developed meanings, despite the recognition that *at a certain level* one might see these meanings to be relative to a particular culture. For the purpose of curriculum development, however, it is most important to determine at what level this questioning and this restructuring of reality is logically possible. For the movement towards an 'integrated' as opposed to a 'collection' code (to use Bernstein's words, 1971) would seem to arise from an epistemological position in which the entire construction of reality is the product of a negotiation between teacher and learner, rather than of the learner being introduced to a public world of meaning already awaiting him.

Summary

SECTION I

Socialization in one form or another is seen more and more as an aim of education. It is felt that schools should prepare pupils for adult life, citizenship, work, social relationship and so on. Such is the message of Newsom and subsequent Schools Council working papers. Nonetheless, beneath this umbrella one might see quite distinct objectives:

(i) learning about local society;
(ii) a disciplined study from the viewpoint of the social sciences;
(iii) moral education;
(iv) training in the 'correct' social attitudes.

SECTION 2

I have criticized such objectives mainly as follows. Firstly, to learn about your local society is very often a narrow factual study that does not have built in the critical outlook and standards of comparison that are features of education. Secondly, these quite distinct objectives are confused so that descriptive and explanatory studies are interlaced with prescriptive and evaluative propositions about attitudes and values. Thirdly, socialization is often seen as a function or use to which education is put rather than an intrinsic feature of education; it is seen as a reason for, or function of, education rather than as an educational aim.

SECTION 3

To meet this sort of criticism I have suggested that socialization might be seen rather as an explication of what we mean by education in so far as 'understanding', 'knowledge', 'thought' are intelligible only within a social form of life in which the individual participates and through which his own awareness and critical approval are formed.

SECTION 4

At the same time, to recognize the public, and thereby social, nature of thinking does not mean that the development of a particular way of thinking is arbitrary or open to fundamental change. There are both logical and practical limits to what can be meant by the individual reconstructing his world or reality.

Further Reading

SECTION 1

In the appendix there is a list of Schools Council projects and working papers and of other projects that make suggestions or recommendations for, or offer examples of, social studies courses. One should look at Working Paper No. 11 and some of the contributions to Working Papers Nos 12 and 22 to get some idea of the banality to which these suggestions reduce themselves. Working Paper No. 39 goes some way towards improving the rather tarnished Schools Council image in this area.

Two books which give details of school based attempts to introduce social studies are edited by Vincent Rogers (1968) and Irvine Smith (1968). Charmian Cannon (1964) treats the history of the social studies movement in England in considerable detail.

SECTION 2

Details of MACOS are not easy to come by. Bruner (1966) gives an initial introduction and the Education Development Centre (1969) has issued an evaluation report. Further information, would be obtainable from C.A.R.E., University of East Anglia, Norwich. Further background to the Humanities Curriculum Project is given at the end of John Elliott's essay.

A very useful attempt to outline some of the essential meanings and principles that could be the focus of a social studies curriculum is in Schools Council Working Paper No. 39. Hilda Taba (1967) attempts to identify essential concepts and principles, and uses the analysis provided by Bruner's (1963) spiral curriculum. Social studies, as an integrating or core element in the curriculum, is carefully examined by both Taba (1962) and Smith, Stanley and Shores (1957). A functionalist analysis of education by sociologists is, of course, best illustrated by reference to the Durkheim (1956). It is, in broad outline, the sort of analysis which is approved of by empirical sociologists in the pre-ethnomethodological era. For a statement and stylish criticism of this conception of education read Oakeshott (1972). A valuable critique of Durkheim and analysis of socialization and education is provided by P. White (1972).

SECTION 3

The best analysis of 'aim' in education is Peters (1973). The public, rule-following, and thereby social character of language, its differentiation, and its relation to different 'forms of life', has been explored very fully by contemporary philosophy, despite its recent promulgation (albeit in a very different way) as an exciting discovery by sociologists. Read in this connection Wittgenstein (1958) part I, especially those sections concerned with rule following and with 'forms of life'. A readable introduction to all this is Pole (1958). An application of these ideas to society is to be found in Winch (1958).

For a thorough treatment of the American tradition, read Dewey *Democracy and Education* (1916) especially chapters 7, 14, 19, 21, 22, and 23; Kilpatrick (1933) or indeed Cremin (1961). Aristotle has something relevant to say: see *Politics III*, 4, 5, 7 and *V*, 9, 9.

SECTION 4

The two books on sociology of knowledge recently published are those edited by Young (1971) and Filmer (1972). In *Education for Teaching*, Autumn 1972, there are three articles on this subject: one summarizing the general theory, one applying it to education courses and one criticizing its philosophical assumptions. In the third article I gave a more extensive criticism of its philosophy than I could have done in this essay. (See Gorbutt, 1972.)

Aims and Objectives in a Social Education Curriculum

HUGH SOCKETT

Introduction

Social education may be regarded as a recent phenomenon in English education. Paradoxically few schools would deny that they did any social education. For as communities they have norms of behaviour to which they expect their members to adhere. In the post-Newsom Report era and more particularly with the change in the school leaving age, talk about social education has considerably increased. There are not only national and local projects, but many individual teachers are trying to devise 'relevant' programmes for children leaving school at the minimum age. Frequently these courses are called 'social education courses'. This avoids the stigma of 'Newsom courses' (and why they are called that must be a mystery to many pupils); it is clear affirmation of 'separate, but equal', non-academic but equally worthwhile; it marks an attempt to build up 'an education that makes sense'. The heterogeneity of courses which run under this label makes it difficult to stipulate what social education *must* be, though most of them contain some moral education, some local and social studies and frequently some residential experience and community service, though there are considerable differences of approach.

The inspiration of the Newsom Report, together with the pressures of raising the school leaving age (RoSLA), has fostered this curriculum reform; it may be seen as a response to Sir Fred Clark's (Clarke, 1943) wartime challenge that in the post-war years the schools would have to build up a 'genuine popular philosophy of education'. Clarke saw the school as a tool in the programme of social reconstruction which would be needed, and this idea is apparent in many programmes. One may be more or less sanguine about the continuing development of such curricula, once the pressures of RoSLA have worn off; the dynamic and innovatory may well become the static and conventional.

However, such curriculum innovation is being conducted at a time when there is considerable research and experiment in the problems of curriculum design and planning. This link between 'social reconstructionism' and curriculum design and planning was a feature of American education in the 1920s and 1930s (see Further Reading Section 1 (i)). The revolt against the enervating elementary education curriculum brought into consideration both problems of the content of the curriculum and how best to tackle the problems of teaching. Some, like Franklin Bobbitt and W. W. Charters, argued for vocational education and training. They planned curricula with objectives drawn from a detailed analysis of particular jobs: Charters for example published a curriculum book, *Selling Retail*. Others, like Harold Rugg and Frank Bonser, had a wider view of the content of the curriculum but still wanted precise and detailed planning of objectives. In 1926 the key phrase was 'maximal growth at minimal expense', a combination of Deweyan ideas about education as growth and a scientific approach to educational problems moderated by efficiency considerations drawn from industrial models of planning.

While 1927 saw the publication of an important and hopeful Yearbook on *The Foundations of Curriculum Development* (National Society for the Study of Education), the political events of the next twenty years prevented strong developments in curriculum experiments—the depression, the war, post-war administrative difficulties, the Korean war, and McCarthyism. The shock to American political and educational sensibilities administered by the launching of the Sputnik in 1956 directly contributed to massive funding of curriculum research and development whose threads had been preserved over the fallow years by researchers like Ralph Tyler and Hilda Taba. The 1960s in the U.S.A. therefore saw independent curriculum development and research. Thus as the curriculum reform movement in this country got under way after the establishment of the Schools Council in 1964, there was a considerable body of curriculum research on which British reformers could trade. How much contact there has been, how great American influence is, will be a matter for historians to discover. Most clearly, however, one project (the North-West Regional Curriculum Development Project) has its theoretical roots in American research (see further Reading, Section 1 (ii)).

Perhaps there is little general awareness of American or British curriculum work among British teachers reforming their curriculum. Curriculum planning and design problems have been conspicuous by their absence from initial training courses for teachers and until recently from advanced courses as well. Thus consideration of changes in the content of the curriculum have not generally been matched by serious enquiry into how teachers ought to plan their courses. The message of the curriculum planners has got through to the extent that as teachers we would be rather self-conscious these days about planning what we do without first deciding what our objectives are. This is in marked contrast to the 'bad old days' when the head or the head of department drew up a syllabus and told us to get on with it. However this situation is changing. There are now one or two British texts, for example, Wiseman and Pidgeon's book on curriculum evaluation (Wiseman and Pidgeon, 1970), which puts forward a particular view of planning. On the other hand there are numerous texts containing suggestions for changes in content—particularly in the social studies area (see Further Reading, Section 1 (iii)).

There is, however, a short document specifically on planning a curriculum in social education which links curriculum planning research with the post-Newsom reconsiderations of content. This is Schools Council Pamphlet No. 5, written by Philip Taylor (Taylor, 1970) whose other work in the curriculum area is well known. In this pamphlet he outlines a procedure for planning a curriculum to meet the aims which Working Paper No. 27 suggests. This document contains primarily analyses, suggestions for content and method without advocating a particular curriculum framework. The Taylor procedure therefore forms an admirable focus for considering both problems of social education and problems of curriculum planning. In this paper I propose to do three things. First I want to set out Taylor's procedure and deal in depth with one major difficulty, common to all those who adopt his approach. Secondly I propose to pick out certain problems which arise for social education in using this particular procedure for planning a social education curriculum, difficulties which may be generalized across social education and which are not merely problems which arise from adopting this procedure. Thirdly I will set out certain considerations which need to be taken into account when planning social education. Whereas in the first two sections I will be concerned with curriculum objectives, in the third section I will make a case for the importance of considering our aims.

SECTION 2

1. *'Curriculum Planning for Compensatory Education—a suggested Procedure'*

This is the title of Professor Taylor's pamphlet. He is careful to indicate that these are suggestions, not prescriptions, but the form of the suggestions for planning is sufficiently orthodox in curriculum theory for us to take them as a planning model. It will be sensible to set out first the procedure and to set out the various difficulties which it must face. One of these difficulties, the problem of 'prespecification' will then be examined in detail.

Taylor's suggested procedure

Taylor takes Working Paper 27 as his starting-point. Its conclusions he describes as ' worthwhile sentiments: agreement with them is one thing, translating them into practice another. The reality we confront and the ideals we hold seem to a degree incompatible'. Thus we need techniques useful in translating the aims of social education, expressed by the Working Paper as 'Competence, Confidence and Cooperation' into practical educational procedures.

As a planning technique he suggests a threefold division:

(a) *Aim*

A broad statement of educational intention incorporating an attitude to certain values. The main point from Working Paper No. 27 is that a central aim in compensatory education is social education.

(b) *General Objectives*

A translation of aims into statements which convey some idea of the practicalities embedded in the aims and some idea of how these practicalities might be achieved. Thus Working Paper No. 27 gives competence, confidence and cooperation as general objectives and work in groups, reading, writing, drama, art, mathematics and social work as means for achieving these objectives.

Following Ralph Tyler these objectives are broken down into:

(i) *behavioural* components (those characteristics of the pupils it is intended to cultivate: e.g. competence, confidence and cooperation), and (ii) *substantive* components (the means for cultivating the characteristics, e.g. drama).

(c) *Specific objectives*

A further translation of general objectives into statements which indicate the specific characteristics which it is desired to cultivate in pupils and the specific means which are to be the vehicle for their achievement:

1 Specific behavioural components: the particular characteristics of pupil behaviour which it is intended to cultivate and which are congruent with the stated general objectives, e.g. the ability to read a simple story requiring a reading age of 13, i.e. an analysis of competence, then confidence, then cooperation.

2 Specific substantive components—particular means for cultivating the intended pupil behaviour, e.g. kind and style of reading material, content of oral work, the specific nature of the 'group work' setting.

I propose to deal with one major difficulty from this account, namely that of the demand for *prespecification* of the objectives, regarded as critical in curriculum models of this kind.

2. Some problems of the prespecification of objectives

As is implied by Taylor's suggested procedure, the teacher must prespecify the specific objectives in terms of behaviour and content. This means that he is to give a precise description of what the learner is to do after undergoing what we may call a 'learning experience'. One of the complaints with which Popham (Popham, 1969) deals is that such prespecification prevents the teacher taking advantage of other instructional opportunities in the classroom, for he is mainly concerned to see that the learners get to the targets he has outlined. However it may well be the case, as Popham suggests, that the teacher will be able to take advantage more easily of a learner's spontaneous comments. Much will depend on the teacher. What therefore is the difficulty?

The point of prespecification in such detail is to describe the precise response which a child is to make to the stimuli: *a fortiori* the unspecified response is wrong. Logically one cannot prespecify original responses (where 'original' is not equivalent to the response of a genius). As more latitude is given to the interpretation or judgement of the pupil, the less specific the objective becomes. In this sense the teacher has less claim to be citing specific (behavioural) objectives. Moreover, given that such precise prespecification is the goal, it is difficult to know at what level of specificity one ought, as a planner, to stop. Indeed Popham finds this a problem, as does Tyler. In his paper (1966) reviewing developments since the publication of *Basic Principles of Curriculum and Instruction* (Tyler, 1949), Tyler makes the point that the level of generality or specificity required of an objective is a major outstanding problem for the behavioural objectives model. The difficulty is therefore twofold:

(a) that what is prespecified cannot include interpretation or judgement since one cannot know in advance what that will be,
(b) that in planning we have no indication of *how* specific we ought to be.

The notion of prespecification is, however, also connected with the manner of teaching, in other words, with how the content is taught. It is the case, I believe, that prespecifying objectives is intimately connected with *instruction*, as a mode of teaching, and if this is shown to be correct then we must ask how far '*what* is being taught' is an appropriate object of instruction. Many advocates of the behavioural objectives model frequently refer to behavioural objectives as *instructional* objectives. One finds too that teaching machines are sometimes called 'instructional devices', and here one finds an obvious paradigm case of objectives being prespecified.

Instruction as a mode of teaching (given that teaching is a polymorphous concept) has clear affinities with our general use of instruction where we speak of instructions to our solicitors, or of instructing someone to shut the door. When we say 'shut the door', however, this is a command, an order, an imperative. We may say 'I instructed him to shut the door' and this would not imply that I have given him any instructions about *how* to shut the door. But when I instruct someone how to shut the door, I am certainly not inviting him to find out for himself; I am giving him directions, or orders, from which I hope he will learn how to shut doors. Thus we find cricket or swimming instructors constantly talking in imperatives: 'get your elbow higher', 'breathe in now', 'put your feet like this', though their intention is that the pupil shall learn, which our ordinary non-teaching instructions like 'shut the door' do not imply. In cases of instruction in 'cognitive abilities' the imperative may simply be a suppressed 'know ye that'. There is thus an implicit imperative in all our senses of instruction. In the teaching sense the aim is to get someone to learn. But there is also a necessary element of prespecification. We must give instructions which have content, which state what the learner or the person is to do. Without that our instructions are empty, just as our commands are empty without content. Even so, some teachers do exhort their pupils to 'Think, boy!' at which that bewildered expression comes over a child's face which indicates that he doesn't know what he is supposed to do.

There is, therefore, a significant connection in practice between prespecifying what a learner is to do and instruction, as a pedagogical mode. If we now turn to the content, to what is taught, instruction seems to be a sensible mode of teaching in the case of physical skills—playing a cover-drive, cooking an omelette, or dismantling a carburettor. As far as cricket coaching is concerned there is nothing new about the 'behavioural objectives' model: the cover-drive is broken down into a series of movements of the bat and the body in relation to the ball's trajectory. We may safely assume that as far as physical skills are concerned, instruction is commonly used and eminently sensible as a method or mode of teaching.

However there is a *prima facie* case for thinking that in literary and aesthetic activities, in moral education and in perhaps a major part of our theoretical activities too, instruction in this sense is less obviously a generally appropriate method. First let us be clear (a) that there may well be necessary facts and skills in these areas which it would be prudent to teach by instruction and (b) that we could decide to teach those elements alone. How far that would provide an adequate *education* is a further question. Thus if our general aim was to introduce children to Shakespearean literature, and more specifically Hamlet, (see Further Reading Section 2 (i)) one could teach certain techniques of criticism *by instruction* together with a number of facts about who kills, loves, hates or is related to whom. However, it is less clearly the case that we ought to prespecify interpretations of the play or of particular characters, even though the viability of the interpretations or judgements which children may make if the possibilities are left open is a considerable problem in aesthetics. What is true is that unless and until children are given the opportunity to make interpretations and judgements 'of their own' (i.e. where their responses are not prespecified) it is extremely unlikely that they will come to see the 'interpretation' of the play as a significant mode of understanding it, or of understanding literature in general. By prespecifying the interpretation one is giving the child little opportunity to distinguish what is a matter of interpretation and what is a matter of fact. How one understands and interprets the character of Hamlet is more open to disagreement and uncertainty than the fact that he killed Polonius or hated Claudius.

Religious *instruction* of course has been labelled by more or less aggressive secularists as indoctrination, and current curriculum suggestions for R.E. go out of their way to avoid this charge. Moreover, one faces similar problems of instruction and prespecification in moral education. If one takes a moral problem for discussion with children, while it is possible that there may be a 'right' course of action, what is at least crucial in the development of rational moral agents is that different courses of action are examined, and different possibilities argued for. What could it be to prespecify objectives, with behaviour and content divisions, in moral education? Another interesting case is that of the teaching of science. For while one may be able to prespecify the methods a child is to use in a particular experiment, the notion that the *result* of the experiment could be prespecified is anathema to the whole conception of science as testing and validating hypotheses about the empirical world. It is therefore not obvious that prespecification in detail of what the child is to 'think, act and feel' has application across the board in education. Its obvious usefulness and application in skills, or in training, is not shared by its application in theoretical, practical or aesthetic pursuits. Indeed Taylor's application of his procedure to social education indicates precisely the dangers and difficulties in rigid adherence to the procedure outlined above with the demand for precise prespecification.

Thus far I have set out Taylor's procedure. I have then dealt in detail with one problem for the procedure in its advocacy of prespecification, maintaining that there is close practical connection between prespecification and instruction as a teaching method. I have argued that instruction is manifestly suitable for physical skills, but difficult if not impossible to maintain if one wants to get children going on more 'cognitive' pursuits.

Elsewhere a range of criticisms have been directed at the behavioural objectives model (see Further Reading, Section 2 (ii)), not all of them well-directed, and this is not the place to summarize them. Those which seem more promising include the difficulties of the behaviour-content dichotomy, the implied relationships between authority and knowledge, and problems of how a child sees himself when following such a programme.

I have been content to argue against the prespecification of objectives in the terms that Taylor has used them, namely the prespecification of learning outcomes, and the major brunt of the attack on behavioural objectives in the curriculum literature has criticized this prespecification aspect. I have not shown however that there may well be other kinds of objectives, perhaps of a methodological kind, which one could not write down in advance or work to which would make them in some sense objectives. I might for example simply decide to proceed by using a 'discussion' method. Notice however that while I might then call this a 'prespecified objective' it would not be of the form that Taylor or others would recognize as such (see Further Reading, Section 2 (iii)). I want now to show how the rigid application of the tight procedure I have criticized can lead to considerable difficulties in social education.

3. *Taylor's analysis of 'social competence' into roles and skills*

Taylor advocates an analysis of 'social competence' into roles and skills. He suggests that if we aim at 'social competence' then at the general and the specific objectives level we must describe what a socially competent person can do. This we do by describing the social roles a person may be called upon to play, and then enlist the relevant behaviours, in other words, make an inventory of social skills. He suggests the following roles: father, friend, husband, neighbour, employee, trade unionist, citizen, sportsman, consumer, traveller, householder and taxpayer. Each social role, he goes on, if it is to be played with competence, calls for certain social skills and capabilities to be exercised appropriately in certain circumstances. Some of the skills are in the intellectual field, that is, they require use of the mind. Some are in the field of feeling or attitudes and require to be understood by a person if they are to be employed by him effectively.

What are we to make of this suggestion? In the pamphlet Taylor does not attempt to spell out any of the skills which constitute the social roles he mentions, but uses such skills as 'speaking' and 'listening', which as examples are not much help. Nevertheless Taylor is apparently suggesting that we analyse the role of the father into behavioural skills with appropriate contexts set out as specific objectives. But what skills count? Can we give any account of the skills necessary and/or sufficient to being a father? Does he really mean that we select say 'washing' as a skill, and fit in the different contexts, e.g. baby, the car, the crockery, the wife and so on? What criteria for the choice of such skills could we use? The initial difficulty seems to be that the role-concept of father just does not describe any particular skills. This applies equally to friend, neighbour and other 'roles'.

Secondly, this attempted characterization of the role of a father into skills derives partly from the emphasis on the demand for prespecified observable behaviours enshrined in the mechanics of this curriculum planning model. More important, it also fails to distinguish between different role concepts. Take the question of role-concepts first. We speak of plumbing as a trade and the plumber as the tradesman. The trade is constituted by certain highly developed skills together with judgement on technical matters. Furthermore such skills are *necessary* to being a plumber at all. We easily speak of a man's skills as a plumber, even though his job may be that of bank-clerk. It is a skill he can use, if he chooses, and no moral blame would fall on him in ordinary circumstances if he chose not to use his skill this weekend. This is not the case with the concept of father. There are no necessary skills as we have seen: there are no judgements on technical matters, nor is being a father something one could choose not to be this weekend. For, the fact of being a father is not a matter of performing skills, but a matter of having *qua* father certain duties, certain rights and certain obligations (see Further Reading, Section 2 (iv)). No obligations necessarily fall on a plumber as they do on a father, for what we mean by being a *father* (as opposed to merely a procreator) is that *his* children have claims, as does their mother, on him. Refusal to accept those responsibilities may incur moral blame.

Thus one should look at the different roles Taylor outlines, and ask whether the emphasis on skills of competence is not derived from a trade model in which the description of the role consists of a number of necessary and perhaps sufficient *skills*, rather than being derived from a role which is described in terms of rights and duties. The immediate impression is that the obligations of fatherhood are reduced to a 'role we play', (as if it wasn't really serious?) by an account of the skills of the handy father. The outward and visible signs are emphasized through this particular curriculum planning model at the expense of the inward and spiritual graces!

If we now begin to look at the wide range of suggested roles in which we are exhorted to develop social competence, we face not merely the question of whether skills or rights and duties should be used in our understanding of a role. For, whereas the plumber's skills are fairly clear, it is not at all clear which skills, let alone which rights and duties one should stress in the other roles mentioned, nor indeed who has the right to choose them. Who counts as a good employee? The subservient hard worker who knows his place? Who counts as a good trade unionist? One who votes Labour? Is the good consumer the man who spends above his means—as economic growth policies seem to demand? If we take one particular example—the trade unionist—one can really appreciate the difficulties. First we may assume the area of agreement on what counts as a good trade unionist may well be small between a radical and conservative teacher. We face perhaps irreconcilable differences of opinion here on a controversial issue. (An attempt to deal with this kind of problem in teaching has been suggested by the Humanities Curriculum Project, but whatever else may be said about that project it is hardly a paradigm of a behavioural objectives model being applied to the curriculum.) Secondly, even if there were as a matter of fact *agreement* among teachers in a particular school (if they were all radical or all conservative) would they not be bound to open up the possibilities of very different options and opinions for their pupils if they were to give them an *education*? Thirdly, as with the notion of a father, 'skills' in talk of the 'skills of a trade unionist' is not a matter of knowing a few facts and the mechanics of voting or handling a mass meeting, but it implies the ability to make judgements in complex social situations, which of course cannot be prespecified.

From the problems of specifying the skills which would make a child 'socially competent in certain roles' we can see that the danger with the application of this procedure is that it treats social education as straightforward socialization (see Pring's paper in this volume): being a father or a trade unionist is seen as being made up of skills similar to that of repairing a ball-valve. To bring children to terms with the dilemmas, the rights and the duties of their roles simply cannot be treated in this way. A continuous attempt must be made to bring children face to face with the difficulties and problems of their moral and social inheritance, for without that social education is a training in (prespecified) conformity.

Thus, in dealing with objectives which are prespecified on Taylor's model, it is important to be aware of the possible damage to certain kinds of content, and to assess the applicability of the model to the content. My claim is that with this suggested content it is highly inapplicable. It may be applicable to physical skills. Some very much less rigid apparatus, incorporating perhaps process objectives, may well be much more sensible in the case of social education (see Further Reading, Section 2 (v)). It is certain that such models must not be taken as panaceas.

SECTION 3
The Aims of the School and the Aims of a
Social Education Curriculum

So far, I have concentrated almost exclusively on the problems of objectives in the curriculum, first with regard to the prespecification of objectives and second with regard to those objectives as skills and the difficulty of stating the 'skills of a role'. However the general problem raised by the dichotomy between socialization and social education is the problem of our *aim*. Aim seems to be a more general concept than objectives, though I have dealt with their differences elsewhere at some length (Sockett, 1972). In this section I want to pick out important distinctions between the aims of the school and the aims of a formal curriculum in social education which raise further problems for procedures of the kind I have examined as well as more general issues about social education.

As part of a prologue to this section it is important to notice that the word 'curriculum' does not seem to be susceptible to any descriptive definition (see Further Reading, Section 3 (i)). That is, one can find such an extraordinarily wide range of usage that most theorists must begin their work by stipulating the definition they are going to use. Some refer to all the experiences the child undergoes as the curriculum. Some refer to the experiences the child undergoes which the teacher plans as a curriculum. Some call a specific type of plan a curriculum; and so on. For the purposes of this paper I shall call all those experiences a child undergoes in the school the curriculum. This is qualified by the fact that a curriculum may be informal or formal: i.e. teachers deliberately may or may not set up certain experiences. Such curricula may be in specific areas, e.g. social education or French. They may also be planned or unplanned if they are formal, that is, under the teacher's direction.

Working Paper No. 27 emphasizes the existence of the formal and the informal curriculum—of what goes on in the classroom and what happens in the social life of the school. Taylor pays no attention to the latter, and American critics of the behavioural objectives model have pointed out that this failure to take account of the particularity of a school as an individual institution weakens its value as a planning method. Skilbeck (Skilbeck, 1968) in his stress on situational analysis, and Macdonald (Macdonald, 1970) in his evaluation of the Humanities Curriculum Project have emphasized this individuality of schools. There is however an important and interesting problem connected with this. At the beginning of this paper it was noted that few schools would deny having done any social education. Such schools would claim that much of *their* social education was, so to speak, 'extracurricular'. It would appear therefore that, whatever goes on in the formal social education curriculum, there will be social education of some kind—perhaps actually only a meagre socialization—going on in the informal curriculum. To bring out various points about this, it is necessary to look briefly at what institutions are and what we mean by talking about the aims of institutions and the aims of schools in particular.

In spite of Ivan Illich and Everett Reimer, we are saddled with the school as an autonomous, or moderately autonomous unit. We value the autonomy of the school as we value the autonomy of the teacher, because education is concerned with developing the autonomy of the child. Institutions are not natural artefacts, nor are they just buildings, and they cannot be adequately described in terms of their empirical functions. Institutions are what their members conceive them to be, whatever the financial props which support them. Winch (Winch, 1958) points out that we can only understand a society or a social institution by understanding the way its members see the world, the conceptual frameworks within which they operate, the criteria of judgement they use and the 'form of life' they share (see Further Reading, Section 3 (ii)). This is not to deny that many interesting empirical facts can be discovered about institutions, illustrated for example by Goffman's (Goffman, 1961) work on asylums, and, in an educational context by Hargreaves' (Hargreaves, 1967) account of Lumley Secondary School.

Whatever disagreements there may be in staffrooms about the purposes of the school, for the school to exist as an institution there must be a measure of shared understanding and agreement about what the aims of the school are, what the school is for and what the school is. There is no logical difference between these three assertions. The aims of the school describe what the school is and thus what it is for, for as a human institution it can only be described in terms of human purposes. There may be dramatic disagreement on what the school is for, as at Risinghill. In some institutions, for example contemporary infant schools, aims are not made explicit. Indeed they may rarely be discussed for there is a shared conceptual framework for describing the social reality and for making intuitive judgements which do not require extensive aims-oriented discussion. On the other hand new schools, like Countesthorpe (McMullen, 1970) may require considerable discussion of aims, and such discussion is a feature of schools undergoing administrative (and thereby educational) change. But it would be a mistake to see such aims as targets to be reached, as goals to be marked off in their achievement. They are guides for making decisions. They are invariably imprecise. The interpretation given to the aims, particularly in such an open-ended situation as a school, will gain some precision for those working within the institution each time a decision, curricular or otherwise is made (see Further Reading, Section 3 (iii)).

There are, however, further important features of schools as institutions. Like other institutions they rely for much of their working life on precedent and tradition. The more complex they are—and Jackson (Jackson, 1968) has shown how bafflingly complex schools are—the wider and more disparate the goals they pursue, the more necessary working by precedent becomes. To point up the importance of this, let us suppose that we took the view of rational action embedded in the behavioural objectives model seriously in an institution. On this view we have to examine carefully each end we pursue and review the possible courses of action to achieve it. But no institution could work at all if such a full-blooded procedure were adopted. To weigh every action performed in an institution against others possible would prevent an institution ever achieving anything or even getting off the drawing board. Such so-called rational action would be, to put it mildly, irrational. Within an institution therefore there will emerge institutional habits, ways of doing things, modes of procedure which incorporate previous value-decisions made about the best way to do things.

This of course does not merely apply to those with power or authority. For this complexity means that different ways of doing things will appear at different levels and in the different sets of relationships which make up the institution: for instance, between members of staff, between staff and pupils, between pupil and pupil, or as many different sets of role-relationships empirical investigation can reveal. Frequently such ways of doing things are enshrined in ritual and in the older schools the ritual may have simply become vestigial. All these sets of relationships constitute together the social life of the school. The sets may clash. The teacher who demands to know who has written the rude words on the blackboard finds that the norms of loyalty or fraternity between the pupils are at odds with the norms of order in the staff-pupil relationship. Clearly what most head teachers and teachers (and perhaps pupils as well) hope is that such clashes between the differing sets of normative relationships within a school are not as serious as those described by Hargreaves at Lumley. For here there was a considerable measure of value-dissonance between the 'official' norms and those of the 'subculture'. This is crucial for those who are concerned with the problems of RoSLA.

These different sets of relationships with their norms of behaviour therefore enshrine certain values—laudable or despicable. Where there is a Lumley-type situation, the area in which there is agreement or acceptance of shared understanding of aims may be infinitesimal, but even the most hardened member of the sub-culture is prepared to accept, albeit temporarily, some of the norms of order. The problem is either to widen the scope of the school's aims (as is being done in social education curricula) and/or to create a social life in which there is a wider measure of acceptance and understanding of the aims of the school.

The aims of the school then may be said to encapsulate its members' conception of the school, and to act as a guide in making decisions. The way in which such aims are realized could not logically be through a planning procedure such as that Taylor recommends, given our current conception of the school. They are realized both in formal curriculum decisions and in the norms of the social relationships which make the school what it is. Of course this presupposes the school 'as we know it'. Maybe we should obliterate the social life of schools by individual tuition arrangements in which no pupil ever met another, and in which teachers too have no institutional social life. The school might then become a combination between a telephone box and a language laboratory. Given our current conceptions however, this is not the measure of the social reality we call the school.

The aims of the school might be the same as the aims of the curriculum in that wide sense of the term that I have suggested. On the other hand if we qualify the term curriculum as planned, or unplanned, or formal, or informal or a mixture of these, then the aims of the school will be wider than any one of these. Whatever our objectives in such curricula, whether they are prespecified or not, they will be chosen in the light of the aims. Teachers will, if they happen to be planning a curriculum or conducting an unplanned curriculum, be making decisions, interpretations, and judgements which exemplify the explicit or implicit aims of the school.

Taylor, in writing of the curriculum in the context is, of course, referring to the planned learning outcomes and teaching activities directed to those ends. He recognizes that teachers will be working as a team when planning a curriculum of this kind which has 'social education' as its aim. Nevertheless the conception of social education advanced by Working Paper No. 27 is clearly one in which the developing autonomy of the child is highlighted —his competence, confidence and cooperation. This is a plea for autonomy for children not merely *within* the curriculum in Taylor's sense, but within the school *qua* institution as the Working Paper's mention of the informal curriculum indicates. Thus it is as important, if not more important, to see that social education from this point of view is not just a matter of a planning procedure. It applies as much to the informal curriculum as it does to the formal. One can think of no greater recipe for chaos than a curriculum which celebrates autonomy and a school social structure which inhibits and diminishes it.

If this is correct we may wonder whether the formal curriculum in social education is itself necessary. For if the informal curriculum did in fact foster the development of competence, confidence and cooperation, perhaps formal curriculum time would be better spent on other things. This is a problem which we may need to reflect on at length. However, these considerations may lead to the conclusion that, concerned as we are with the problems of providing a curriculum in social education for 'reluctant stayers' (one may supply one's own euphemism), focusing on the problem of curriculum objectives from a planner's stance may be time poorly spent if we have not thought more deeply about the aims of the school and thus about the totality of the social experience that makes a school what it is. It is in this light that we need to think more about our aims.

Summary

SECTION 2

Taylor's suggested procedure for curriculum planning in social education was outlined. The prespecification issue was dealt with in detail, with the suggestion that prespecification (and the instruction that is implied) is inappropriate as a teaching mode for many things we want to teach as well as for much social education work. It was suggested too that on closer examination Taylor's suggestions for the curriculum made with the pre-specification of skills relating to social competence as father, trade unionist, etc., were fundamentally misguided in that they confuse the notion of a 'trade' with that of a 'role'. The cause of this confusion is found in Taylor's cleaving to prespecification and instruction which are suitable only for teaching physical skills.

SECTION 3

Some important considerations about the way we must view institutions if we act within them as members were put forward. Particular stress was laid on the importance of the social life of an institution and the necessary place for tradition and precedent in which aims as values are embedded. Finally some speculations were advanced as to whether, in social education, consideration of the informal curriculum, (and with it more thought about the aims of the school) is not necessary, while detailed thought about curricula is going on. Philip Taylor is suitably modest about his 'suggested procedure', and does not claim to be offering a prescription. Theorists who share his views do not share his modesty. We need to beware of those who offer planning panaceas as much as we need to be sure that what we provide is social *education* and not second-rate socialization.

Further Reading

SECTION I

  (i) An excellent account of the clash between the American elementary tradition with its 'mental discipline' panacea and John Dewey and his followers is well documented in the 26th Yearbook of the National Society for the Study of Education (1927) Volume II. The main interest lies in the way in which Harold Rugg, the editor, a committed social reconstructionist, criticizes both positions and begins to outline a curriculum theory which has influenced Curriculum Theory considerably.

  (ii) A brief account of this project is a paper by Allan Rudd (1970).

  (iii) A clear and concise book, not much influenced by curriculum theory as such, is Philip and Priest (1965). For an excellent review of social science problems in teaching, see Morrisett (1967) and a paper by Hanvey (1971).

SECTION 2

  (i) Lawrence Stenhouse (1970–1971) takes up this case in his paper. He raises in particular questions about the appropriateness of regarding content 'instrumentally'. However his assumption that Hirst's formula for rational curriculum planning is to be regarded as a tight behavioural objectives model is perhaps a misunderstanding.

  (ii) Critical articles include the Stenhouse paper mentioned above, Atkin (1970) and Steinberg (1972).

  (iii) John White (1972) has attempted to characterize different senses in which an objective may be behavioural. See also Sockett (1973).

  (iv) A classic view of this conception of a 'role', though he would not have called it that, is to be found in Bradley (1876).

  (v) See, for example, Parker and Rubin (1966).

SECTION 3

  (i) For discussion of definitions of curriculum, see Scheffler (1960) Ch. 1.

  (ii) Winch (1958) makes a classic attack on positivistic sociology. Of particular relevance is his section on 'understanding social institutions' (Chapter III, part 6).

  (iii) I have tried to spell this out more clearly (Sockett, 1972).

3

The Humanities Project on 'People and Work' and the Concept of Vocational Guidance*

JOHN ELLIOT

SECTION I

The Concept of Vocational Guidance

Whatever contemporary advocates of vocational guidance in schools and institutions believe to be central elements of the concept, I take it these should not include:

(a) Training in the skills or 'know how' required by particular types of work. There now appears to be a general consensus among employers that this kind of training is best left to them.

(b) Training in skills or 'know how' required to get a job, e.g. getting information about jobs, writing letters of application, filling in forms, and 'how to get through the interview successfully'.

(c) Acquiring information about employment opportunities and particular kinds of job available.

Although these elements may be important aspects of vocational guidance in certain contexts, when they have all been accomplished, the central task of vocational guidance is not achieved. I assume that central to the concept of vocational guidance now being advocated is the idea of helping pupils and students to make, in some sense, rational decisions, with respect both to the kind of work they will do, and to the social situations they will encounter at work. These decisions are not merely technical decisions about how best to execute a particular job-task, or get the job that is wanted, but decisions which often involve controversial social and political values. A technical decision involves the choice of a course of action in the belief that it will be the most effective way of realizing certain valued objectives.

*This essay represents a personal point of view and not necessarily that of the Project's central team. It is a revision of an article previously published in *The Career Teacher*, Spring 1973.

But in a social context our choices are rarely as simple as this; the objectives are not always sufficient criteria for justifying a person's choices. For example, a man wishes to avoid leaving property with death duties payable after his death, and knows this can be done legally if he hands his property over to his wife and children. But he refuses to do this in the belief that this act would constitute an act of dishonesty. Again, the decision to apply to 'go down the mines with Dad' rather than to apply for university admission is not simply a technical one. For to apply for university might in a certain social context constitute an act of 'betrayal' towards a working class value of solidarity. Similarly, the decision to engage in work which is unchallenging and which demands little commitment, for the sake of pursuing one's hobby wholeheartedly, may be viewed by upholders of the protestant work ethic as sheer 'laziness' and 'irresponsibility'. In other words, in social situations conceptions of one's moral and political obligations as well as technical criteria place limits on what can be considered legitimate means to ends. In such situations an understanding of people's activities presupposes the application of moral, social and political criteria. They are not neutral, value-free descriptions of human conduct. Inasmuch as people's activities in social situations can be viewed from the standpoint of different forms of social life embodying different evaluative outlooks they raise controversial issues. What from one point of view appears to be a rational and good choice from another appears to be an irrational and bad choice.

If vocational guidance is centrally concerned with getting students into the position of being able to make rational decisions about desirable courses of action in publicly controversial areas like work, then it faces the problem of how to proceed in an educational context. 'Guidance' implies that some influence can be brought to bear by teachers and counsellors which will help students make rational decisions. It is the nature of this 'influence' which must be a central problem for vocational guidance. Are the students to be 'guided' towards a view of the work situation which can be located within a middle rather than a working class ethic? Are they to be 'guided' towards a conception of work which makes it a necessary vehicle of self-realization rather than an instrument of self-realization in other spheres of life? If we brought teachers and counsellors concerned with vocational guidance together to discuss such questions to what extent would they disagree? I would hazard the guess that the disagreement would be considerable. They would find their disagreements rooted in the different evaluative outlooks they bring to their understandings of acts and situations within the field of work. What counts as a rational course of action in a situation for some will not appear to be rational for others, because what is to count as a rational decision will depend on the different evaluative standards located within different moral, social and political outlooks. Moreover, there is no way of standing outside these points of view and agreeing about what constitutes a rational decision from the standpoint of some neutral criterion.

Does this mean, then, that there is no guarantee that teachers and counsellors will ever be able to agree about what constitutes vocational guidance; different groups should merely go their own way, defining their role from the standpoint of their own moral, social and political outlooks? If the answer is 'yes' then it opens the way to vocational guidance becoming an ideological battlefield for the 'hearts and minds' of students. And this raises two problems. Firstly, don't people in public positions in our society have a responsibility to respect the divergence of view which exists among different sections of the general public, for instance, between parents, employers and students? Even if by some happy coincidence all the teachers and counsellors brought together did share a common evaluative outlook this could not be guaranteed in society at large. Secondly, since it would be logically impossible for a teacher or counsellor to demonstrate to a student that a course of action which is rational from one outlook is more *rational* than an alternative course which is rational from a different outlook, he could not aim at getting him to choose one rather than the other, without at the same time encouraging him to do so purely out of deference to his authority position rather than by reasoned conviction.

These two points are not unconnected. Teachers and counsellors have an educational responsibility to foster their students' rational capacities. When there are publicly agreed procedures for rationally resolving problems it is possible to foster these capacities by demonstrating the difference between true and false, valid and invalid, right and wrong solutions. But when there is public disagreement on what would count as a rational solution to a problem, as there is with respect to many practical problems connected with the work situation, these capacities cannot be fostered by the teacher or counsellor taking sides and thereby supporting one position rather than another. This is why educators are under an obligation to respect different views based on different standards of reasoning. It follows from this that there is something contradictory in the suggestion that people responsible for vocational guidance in schools should use their authority position as teachers to influence students' vocational and work decisions in directions they personally favour, for in exercising such influence they are fostering authority-dependent decisions rather than rational ones.

On the basis of these arguments one might be tempted to draw the conclusion that vocational guidance in the way I originally defined it is impossible. If the teacher or counsellor has no agreed public standards of reasoning to appeal to in the activity of guidance, how can he help students make rational decisions about their work? Surely, one might suggest, there is little positive influence he can legitimately bring to bear? Perhaps it would be better if he completely refrained from influencing his students' decisions in any way, and limited his concept of vocational guidance to the sort of things mentioned at the beginning of this article. This position could be described as complete passivity with respect to the moral, social and political decisions students will be required to make in the field of work.

However, I would like to suggest, as a result of my experience on the Humanities Curriculum Project (see Stenhouse *et al.*, 1970), that there is a way of bringing some educationally legitimate and positive influence to bear on the way students think about socially controversial acts and situations in the field of work. This might have some relevance to attempts to reach an agreed conception of vocational guidance. Central to this conception would be the idea that 'influence' or 'guidance' can be exercised in a form which is *procedurally neutral*. The term 'procedural' is intended to indicate that the 'neutrality' being picked out is not to be equated with *complete passivity* or *negative neutrality*, towards the decisions which face students. In other words, there is a way of exercising positive influence or guidance in socially controversial areas which does not involve using one's authority position as an educator to take sides in favour of one controversial evaluative position rather than another.

SECTION 2
Controversial issues and the procedures of the Humanities Project

The Humanities Project, under the direction of Lawrence Stenhouse, began in 1967 to help adolescents develop their understanding of morally, socially and politically controversial issues. These issues were classified in terms of the kinds of acts and situations which people disagree about in our society, e.g. War and Society, Education, Family, Relations between the Sexes, Poverty, Law and Order, Living in Cities and People and Work. The phrase 'controversial issues' looks a bit odd since by definition all issues are controversial. But this prefix tends to pick out certain kinds of issues from others. Some disputes over desirable courses of action can be accounted for merely as disputes about the likely consequences of courses of action. Once people are agreed that there is sufficient evidence for predicting a particular set of consequences they will agree about what ought to be done. Such issues presuppose that disputants agree on the sort of facts, which if established, will settle the issue in a rational way. One understands these issues when one grasps both the agreed standards of evaluation they are based on, and the assumption this involves that a rational consensus of judgement must be possible. But there are other kinds of dispute which involve not only disagreements about the consequences of particular courses of action, but disagreements about the sort of consequences which would count as good reasons for adopting one course of action rather than another. An understanding of these issues involves the realization that it makes no sense to say that such issues must be resolved on the basis of a rational consensus, since what is to count as a rational solution is part of the problem. This realization is brought about by understanding the issue in terms of the different sorts of reasons which are at stake; it necessitates coming to view the problematic act or situation from the standpoint of different moral, social or political points of view.

Not all value-issues in the area of work are of the second kind. There is a considerable area of consensus about the kind of considerations which have to be taken into account when making decisions. There are therefore some kinds of decisions facing students in the area of work, where teachers and counsellors might be able to muster sufficient evidence to demonstrate the desirability of certain choices rather than others. But this presupposes that the act or situation in question falls unambiguously under some publicly agreed standard. The Humanities Project is not primarily concerned with such issues. Rather it is concerned with those enduring and persistent issues of the second kind, which are suggested by the prefix 'controversial'. Here disputants may agree about which considerations are relevant, but disagree about which have overriding force when they conflict. Or each side may have different standards of relevance.

Within the field of work we may well find that issues about 'the role of unions', 'strikes', 'equal pay for women', 'the relationship between work and leisure, or work and family life', 'the value and status of different kinds of work', involve not only disputes about the facts but fundamental differences in people's overriding evaluative outlooks.

How can an understanding of such 'controversial' issues arising out of work situations help students make rational decisions in these areas? Some contemporary philosophers have answered the question in the following way:

'In order to hold a moral viewpoint, to understand it, expound it and defend it, it may be necessary to take account of the moral viewpoints of one's opponents.' (Phillips and Mounce, 1969, chapter 9, p. 108.)

'. . . that in dealing with others we ought to reveal in our attitudes a realization that the rules in terms of which they act may also be valid for us.' (Downie and Telfer, 1969, chapter 1, section 5.)

In other words, if a decision is to be a rational one the person making it ought to take into account alternatives to their own ways of evaluating an act or situation. A necessary, but not sufficient, condition of making objective judgements and decisions about publicly controversial kinds of acts and situations in the field of work is an understanding of the nature and structure of the public issues they raise. It is not sufficient, because such an understanding will not necessarily reveal to the student the direction along which a solution to his problems can be found. Indeed, it involves the realization that, since the issue involves a conflict between different standards of objectivity, he not only has to commit himself to a rational course of action, but make a personal commitment to a view of what in these circumstances is to count as a rational course of action. Neither teachers, counsellors, or society in general can make this commitment for him.

If, central to our conception of vocational guidance, is the view that students ought to be helped to make rational decisions by developing their understanding of the controversial issues in the area of work, then we have a view of 'guidance' and 'influence' which is *neutral*. 'Influencing' or 'guiding' students towards this understanding must involve the teacher or counsellor *qua* educator in deliberately refraining from misusing his authority position by attempting to 'influence' or 'guide' the students in the direction of a commitment to a particular position, e.g. his own. To attempt the latter would involve discouraging students from giving equal consideration to divergent views and neglecting to protect divergence existing both in society and among his students. If the teacher or counsellor is to aim at developing an understanding of controversial issues he must encourage 'equality of consideration' and 'protect (not encourage) divergence'. If he is not 'guiding' or 'influencing' according to these procedural principles he cannot be aiming to develop his students' understanding of issues. Thus the deliberate withholding of certain kinds of 'influence' or 'guidance' is a necessary condition of being able to exercise those influences which facilitate understanding and place students in a position to make rational decisions in the area of work. This 'deliberately refraining from' for the sake of educationally legitimate influence is what is meant by *procedural neutrality*. It is certainly not to be equated with *complete passivity* or *negative neutrality*. It involves passivity towards some aspects of an issue for the sake of exerting positive 'influence' and 'guidance' with respect to other aspects.

As well as the principles of 'neutrality', 'equality of consideration', and 'protecting divergence', the aim of developing understanding also implies the desirability of *discussion* rather than *instruction* as the basic educational activity. To understand the issues, disputants must examine and reflect on different arguments and reasons with a view to assessing their intelligibility, and this can only be done by understanding one's own values and attitudes and exploring the relationship between these and other people's.

For example, a middle class student can come to appreciate the force that considerations like 'class solidarity' carry for the working class student by reflecting on the importance he himself ascribes to considerations like 'family loyalty' and 'fraternity'. Since they are all members of a particular society there will be aspects of people's conflicting reasons which are similar as well as different. It is this fact which makes understanding possible, at least to some degree.

The kind of discussion activity required by the aim of developing understanding will be very different from that which is appropriate to the solution of purely technical issues, or other issues which presuppose the possibility of consensus. Purely technical disagreements are about the most efficient means to agreed ends. For example, two people may disagree about the most effective way of avoiding an accident on a sharp corner approached at sixty miles an hour. But this disagreement is based on agreement about the undesirability of accidents. Technical disagreements presuppose an agreed criterion against which different arguments can be criticized and defended. Similarly, with issues about matters of fact, when there is agreement on what evidence would support the truth of some arguments rather than others. With all these issues discussion assumes the possibility of a rational consensus and appropriately takes the form of vigorous argument (defence and criticism). But a discussion aimed at developing understanding of controversial issues must involve a reflective exploration of acts and situations from the standpoint of the different standards on which disputants base their defence and criticisms of each other's positions, rather than the activity of defence and criticism itself. Lively argument where disputants get nowhere because they argue from very different premises may give the teacher or counsellor a glow of pleasure at getting such keen and passionate involvement from his students, but if he is genuinely concerned with developing their understanding of issues he will do better to encourage the less lively, slower-paced, and more reflective activity of trying to understand different outlooks.

So far I have tried to explore the relevance of the aims and teaching principles of the Humanities Project for the concept of vocational guidance. If the central aim of vocational guidance is helping students make rational decisions about publicly controversial acts and situations in the field of work, this implies developing their understanding of issues through the medium of a reflective discussion in which the teacher or counsellor encourages equality of consideration for divergent views, and protects them.

The teacher or the counsellor will be trying to get students to understand the range and depth of public discussion in the field of work. And he cannot realistically expect this range and depth to be represented in the groups he deals with. If the students are to develop their understanding of an issue they will need, at various points in their inquiry, to discuss evidence of the different views people in our society hold on controversial sorts of acts and situations. These views may be embodied in a piece of literature; a poem; a photograph; a film; a folksong; an extract from an interview; or an historian's account of, say, the Peterloo massacre. Students may need to go out and observe people at home or at work, and bring back their evidence for discussion and analysis in the group. ('Work experience' programmes are a marvellous vehicle for collecting such data.) On the other hand, people may be asked to visit the group as 'evidence' and, instead of delivering a boring and often untruthful account of their work experience to a large number of students (followed by the odd question and 'finish'), have their experience and perspectives explored on the students' own terms.

In the Humanities Project resource collections of 'evidence' were prepared by the central team to support teachers who wished to mount discussions on controversial issues. These were edited with the needs of teachers aiming at an understanding of controversial issues in mind. They were then sent to the project's thirty-six experimental schools where they were used by groups of teachers, who having received some training in the procedures, were exploring problems of mounting this kind of discussion-based inquiry with adolescents. After receiving feedback from these groups about the problems of using the archive, and after visiting classrooms to observe for themselves, the editors in the central team re-edited the resource collections for general publication.

SECTION 3
The 'People and Work' Resource Compilation

One of my own tasks as a member of the central team of the project was to edit a resource compilation to support classroom inquiries in the area of 'People and Work'. (See Elliott, 1969.) The aims of the activity and the form of the classroom procedure it implied had to be constantly borne in mind during the editing process.

The first problem that had to be faced was how to develop some way of structuring the archive which would permit flexibility of use. One was servicing an inquiry rather than an instructional procedure, led by a teacher-chairman, who, once an issue had been raised and defined for investigation, saw his task as responding helpfully to the discussion as it was initiated and developed by the students themselves. This is a radically different approach to the traditional one in which the students follow and respond to an 'agenda' which is controlled and determined by the teacher. The teacher must see that part of his task is to be a resource consultant, who influences the discussion by providing 'evidence' for the group to consider at appropriate points in the inquiry. The classroom procedure I have outlined would, for example, require the teacher to introduce 'evidence' for any of the following reasons:

1 to deepen the exploration of a particular view;
2 to introduce a new perspective on a problem when the discussion begins to 'run out of steam' or 'goes round in circles';
3 to represent a view which the students have not considered, or to support the exploration of a minority view which is not adequately represented in the group;
4 to sharpen the definition of a view offered in the group by asking its proponents to face critical evidence;
5 to offer concepts which would clearly be helpful to the discussion;
6 to help students make their own points of view explicit, both for themselves and others, by introducing material whose interpretation must inevitably depend on their own evaluative outlook;
7 to help students explore and discuss a highly personal issue through an impersonal medium, thus protecting the students' right to privacy.

As well as exercising some influence over the inquiry in these ways, the teacher would also be required to exercise the following functions:

1 ensuring that questions are asked and problems posed about 'evidence';
2 ensuring that students' ideas and their relationship to each other are clarified;
3 helping students to monitor the main lines of development in discussion;
4 ensuring that the discussion is relevant to the issue;
5 encouraging the students to use and build on each other's ideas;
6 helping the students to raise and define issues for inquiry and to decide on priorities;
7 ensuring that questions are asked which provide intellectual stimulus and encourage reflective self-criticism.

The structure of the compilation had to be of the kind which helped the teacher locate relevant 'evidence' quickly. He would not know at the beginning of a session what would be required, since he is not so much 'influencing' or 'guiding' by predetermining the course of events, but by responding to events as they are initiated by students. Organizing material according to some sequential pattern was not possible.

One way of organizing such a compilation would have been around the public issues which are actually raised in the area of 'People and Work'. However, we decided against this for the following reason: it is doubtful that a student will find an issue problematic unless it is one he can relate to his own experiences in some way, and this will involve formulating the issue in his own terms. It does not necessarily follow from this that issues should be raised by students without any help from the teacher. The latter has a responsibility to help students shape and define an issue which can serve as the focus for a coherent inquiry. But the whole subsequent enterprise will be futile if the students do not in some way come to see an issue as posing a problem or dilemma for them. Many teachers make the mistake of thinking of inquiry merely in terms of understanding (or solving) a problem. They place an issue they believe to be controversial before a group, but the inquiry does not get under way because the students fail to see it as a problem.

On these grounds we felt it unwise to structure the 'evidence' around issues defined in terms which are personally meaningful to the editor. Instead, bearing the aim of the inquiry in mind, a 'map' of the field of 'People and Work' was devised under eight major categories. The main criterion for delineating these 'organizing categories' was their relevance to any inquiry into controversial acts and situations within the area of work. The eight categories were:

A. The meaning of work for the worker

This category functions as an organizing centre for:

  (i) material which presents differing views of either work in general or particular kinds of working situations;
 (ii) material which presents examples of human behaviour in work situations, and which could form the basis of an inquiry into different attitudes, motives, etc.;
(iii) material which represents examples of how sociologists, psychologists, historians, etc., proceed in understanding human behaviour in terms of motives, attitudes, etc.

B. Social Institutions and work values
Family, Education, Politics, Religion

This category functions as an organizing centre for exploring the function of institutions in determining human attitudes and values in relation to work. The material could be of two sorts:

  (i) raw source material from visuals (photographs, paintings, cartoons, advertisements, etc.), films, autobiographies, drama, poetry and literature, which could help students formulate and test their own hypotheses.

(ii) Examples of how enquirers within the behavioural sciences proceed to formulate hypotheses and test them.

C. Social Stratification and the meaning of work

Focuses on the hypothesis that values and attitudes in work situations can be correlated with social class differences.

D. The working environment and its impact on the worker

Focuses on the impact of working conditions on the attitudes, interests and emotions of individuals and groups. Material falls into the two categories outlined in B.

E. Possible variables influencing choice of work and opportunities within it

This category functions as an organizing centre for material suggesting that certain conditions determine or limit an individual's choice of work and subsequent opportunities. Material falls into the two categories outlined in B.

F. Obligations and rights in the working situation

Focuses on the moral problems which human relationships at work present. What rights should different individuals and groups have in the working situation, and what kind of obligations should they acknowledge? This category functions as a centre for:

(i) documenting moral problems in the work situation through the selection of case-studies, autobiographies, interviews and extracts from novels and plays;

(ii) the presentation of different viewpoints on such problems as the role of trade unions, strikes, relationships between employers, management and workers, decision-making responsibilities, etc.;

(iii) how behavioural scientists and historians explain industrial disputes.

G. Conceptions of masculinity and femininity in the working situation

Focuses on the attitudes of men and women towards each other in the working situation. This category functions as a centre for:

(i) documenting different viewpoints on the role of men and women at work;

(ii) presenting examples of male-female relationships at work, that could form the basis of an enquiry into attitudes, interests and emotions.

H. The relationship between work and other human activities

This category functions as an organizing centre for exploring the interaction between the various out-of-work activities individuals and groups engage in, and work itself. Material falls into the two categories outlined in B.

It was hoped that such a structure would help teachers and counsellors locate relevant evidence as quickly as possible. In the published compilation (see Elliott, 1972) the evidence is numbered and the numbers relevant to each category are recorded in the teachers' handbook, which also contains a brief synopsis of each piece of 'evidence'.

Within the structure outlined we tried to select 'evidence' with the following considerations in mind:

Coverage

The compilation should provide at least some material that could service an enquiry into any controversial value-issue raised. However, a collection cannot realistically aim to give complete coverage. Further material will be required through research by both students and teachers. The compilation is a foundation collection and should be supplemented, modified and expanded as time goes on by teachers and students in their own situations.

Balance

One of the most difficult and important tasks of editing this kind of compilation is to provide a balance of viewpoints, attitudes and interests. It is hoped that in the overall compilation a particular bias does not stand out as dominant. However, this is an aspiration which is rarely achieved. One way teachers can initially test for bias is to read and discuss the materials with colleagues. If everyone agrees on a particular bias then it is likely that the editor has fallen short and the materials will need to be supplemented at an early stage. However if there is disagreement over bias then the teacher can have some confidence in the compilation's capacity to support a variety of views and attitudes.

Depth

Since the aim is to develop students' understanding there was need for a compilation which to some extent can sustain this development in depth.

An editor has to take into account the desirability of acquiring new concepts and a deeper and richer understanding of those already acquired. When looking at the compilation for the first time the more difficult material may stand out. But it should be considered in the light of what students may be capable of in the future, rather than what they can cope with now. Whether students get anything of value out of the material largely depends on the teacher's sense of timing and his understanding of his students' needs at various stages of an inquiry. Most of the 'difficult' material is organized according to the concepts of particular disciplines. *In order to make this material easier to cope with the key sections are blocked off and long extracts are frequently divided into short subsections.* This enables the teacher to focus students' attention on a particular block or sub-section which may be relevant to the inquiry. He need only go on to the other parts if they become relevant subsequently to the issue being explored. About twenty-five per cent of the compilation is material of this kind.

Accessibility

Most of the 'evidence' should be of the kind which can be explored at a number of different levels. It should be accessible to students across the ability range, at the initial stages of an inquiry, and also capable of being explored at considerable depth. Films, visuals, poems, extracts from novels and plays (perhaps on tape), and taped interviews and folk songs, are 'evidence' of this kind. They represent over fifty per cent of the compilation (excluding films), and should be accessible in some degree to 'limited' students. There are, in addition, twenty-seven pieces of journalism, a conflict game, and a number of case studies.

Variety

An attempt was made to provide a compilation that contained a diversity of media, e.g. prints, photographs, paintings, tape and film.

As well as this, attention was paid to providing a wide range of different kinds of material in the forms outlined below.

Types of evidence	No. of extracts
Autobiographies, biographies, case studies, diaries, lectures, speeches	13
Drama	9
Journalism	26
Novels	28
Poetry	7

Non-fiction, i.e. history, philosophy, psychology, sociology, statistics, etc.	65
Taped materials, i.e. on tape only	23
Visuals, i.e. photographs, paintings, cartoons, advertisements	66
Recommended film	99
Total	336

Included in the original taped material are interviews and songs. The words of the songs are printed in the handbook.

SECTION 4
An excerpt from classroom discussion

The following excerpt from a student discussion on visual 'evidence' may serve to put some flesh on the sort of procedures I have outlined. The students, who are in their fifth year of secondary schooling, are discussing:

(a) A photograph of 'Factory workers on their way to work'. They are on bicycles and waiting at a level crossing.
(b) A photograph, showing 'Workers leaving the factory gate'. They are running and smiling.

Boy   This is a picture of factory workers on their way to   (1) work, which is from the pack on 'People and Work'. As far as I remember when we had a discussion about this photograph we didn't really get very much from it. It didn't stimulate very much argument.

Boy   Yes, we didn't actually discuss the photograph; we   (2) used it as evidence.

Boy   I think the real point we came to terms with was that it was just a lot of people going to work and they were having to wait at the factory crossing and they were a bit . . .

Teacher   Did we say anything about the relationship between men and their work?

Boy   Not really, no.

Boy   It doesn't show that everyone crowds into work at the last moment and they all clock in without losing money. It just shows that these men may have been held up at

	a level crossing. The person who took this photograph must have tried to conceal the fact but he hasn't done it very successfully because the top of the train going by and the level crossing sign just there . . .	
Teacher	Why do you think he took the photograph?	(3)
Boy	I think he is trying to show that workers are bored with work by the look on their faces.	(4)
Boy	. . . being stopped by a train.	
Boy	It could be a bleak, cold morning in winter and they were a bit fed up with having to wait.	
Boy	I don't think it would be a very cold morning in winter because of their clothes.	
Boy	There's a chap with his shirt undone at the top. Not all the men are wearing caps.	
Teacher	You think the photographer took it to show boredom of the workers?	
Boy	Yes, like so many other photographs of workers. We had some with workers running out at the gates. Just didn't show anything.	
Boy	There was 2005 entitled 'Factory workers leave the factory gate', also by an anonymous bloke . . .	(5)
Boy	I don't think this photograph has much point. It shows people rushing out of a factory gate. It doesn't necessarily mean that they are pleased to get out of their work, it could be that they are pleased that they're going to go where they are going to, because it could be that someone is selling free beer or giving away £5 notes just behind the corner. It doesn't say that does it?	
Teacher	Is it important that you know exactly what happens or is it useful in bringing out certain points about people's attitudes to work?	(6)
Boy	No it doesn't because you don't know what happens. It could be . . . free beer, or it could be that they are glad to get out of work, or it could be their . . .	
Teacher	It is likely that it is. Can one not argue that perhaps it is very unlikely that . . . have you ever known anybody to offer somebody free beer?	
Boy	. . . I mean it might be a bank holiday the next day and they are pleased to get out because of that.	
Teacher	Does that not raise the point that men are pleased not to work?	
Boy	No, not necessarily. That might not happen every day.	

Boy	I mean you just said is it likely that this bloke is waving £5 notes around . . . he could be doing that to fake the photograph couldn't he?
Teacher	Why should the photographer want to fake the (7) photograph?
Boy	Because, I don't know, because he wants to make it look (8) as though workers are oppressed, very upset, they are being done down by the capitalist owners and having to slog away twenty-five hours a day. You know, all this type of thing. It could be completely wrong.
Teacher	Do you believe this to be true—that the men are exploited?
Boy	No I don't. It could be some communist agent who has (9) come across here, takes a picture like this, then takes it back to Russia or China and that, and he'll say, 'Look, all the workers, you know, are oppressed in the factories. When they get out they are so pleased to get out', and it is propaganda.

The students are studying a visual which they have looked at before and which at the time appeared to stimulate little argument (1). One student suggests that whereas previously they had discussed it as evidence, they had not discussed it as a photograph (2). He is followed by a student who implies that in the absence of contextual information it is useless as evidence and this opinion is confirmed by subsequent comments. However, photographs can be seen as evidence in two ways. First, they might be viewed as evidence for the attitudes, feelings, etc. of the people they depict. Secondly, they might be viewed as evidence for the photographer's own attitudes and views. It is probably this sort of distinction student (2) has in mind. The teacher's comment (3) directs the discussion towards considering the views of the photographer, to which student (4) responds by suggesting that he is trying to show how bored the workers are. But subsequent comments return to an examination of the visual as evidence for the workers' actual attitudes. The teacher, probably feeling the problems in this sort of treatment have been adequately explored, tries to bring the discussion back onto the photographer's views by relating it to the comments of student (4). This leads to the suggestion that a similar view is expressed in another photograph by the same man (5). This photograph is again dismissed as evidence for the workers' attitudes. It is interesting that although the reasons for dismissing these visuals as adequate evidence of this kind may be perfectly good ones, it may well be motivated by an evaluative point of view which the students believe to conflict with that of the photographer.

The teacher (6) asks whether it is important to examine these visuals as evidence for people's attitudes to work, and asks the group to return again to the question of the photographer's perspective (7). The student (8) suggests it expresses a view of workers as victims of exploitation, and implies that it is not a valid one. The teacher responds to this by asking a question aimed at getting students to evaluate what they believe to be the photographer's attitude and hence to disclose their own attitudes and viewpoints. The controversial issue implicit in much of this discussion begins to be made explicit (9), (i.e. are factory workers the victims of social and economic exploitation?), together with the conflicting ideological outlooks which might well explain how such issues arise in our society. Which is an illustration perhaps of the value of visual 'evidence' in discussion, not only as evidence for the different viewpoints people in our society bring to bear in their interpretation of human acts and social situations in the field of work, but also as a device for helping students to become more aware of their own points of view, and where they stand on issues which divide society.

Summary

SECTION I

It was argued that, in an educational context, one's conception of vocational guidance must take into account the fact that job-choices and decisions in working situations raise public value issues.

Since in relation to such issues it does not make sense to assert that a rational solution is possible, a problem is posed for vocational guidance. Is it possible for educators to help students make rational decisions without taking sides on public issues?

SECTION 2

Such help is possible by developing students' understanding of the nature and structure of issues in the area of work, since a rational decision must involve taking into account all the sorts of considerations people take to be relevant, if not conclusively so, to a rational decision.

From the teaching aim of 'developing understanding' a number of procedural principles, implied by the aim, were made explicit. Together, the aim and principles provide a set of guidelines for teaching in publicly controversial social areas like work.

SECTION 3

An example was provided of a resource compilation on 'People and Work', edited with the intention of supporting teaching aimed at 'understanding' and based on the principles described.

SECTION 4

Finally, I attempted to show how discussion on 'evidence' can raise, clarify, and promote an understanding of controversial value issues within the area of work.

Further Reading

SECTION 1

A useful resource document on current thinking in the field of vocational education is Schools Council Working Paper No. 40 (1972). For a philosophical analysis of the concept of vocational education read Wall (1967) and my application of this analysis to the relationship between the Humanities Project and vocational education (1969).

SECTION 2

For a deeper treatment of the nature of the kind of value issues which involve conflicting standards of reasoning read Ginsberg (1968); Phillips and Mounce (1969); Beardsmore (1969); Winch 'The Universalizability of Moral Judgements', (1972).

For more clarification of the idea of procedural neutrality in teaching read Stenhouse (1970 and 1971), and for the idea of procedural principles in teaching Peters (1963, chapter 7). Peters' chapter contains seminal insights, the practical implications of which were grasped by Stenhouse alone among the curriculum developers of the 1960s. Some philosophical issues around the concept of teacher neutrality are explored by Bailey and myself (1971 and 1973).

The procedure adopted by the Humanities Project of deriving teaching principles rather than learning outcomes from aims is a different view of curriculum design from planning by objectives. Why the Project rejected the latter procedure is explained by Stenhouse in 'Controversial value issues in the classroom' (1970). Read also Stenhouse's 'Some limitations of the use of objectives in curriculum research planning' (1970–1).

SECTION 3

For an examination of teachers' interpretations of the nature of 'understanding' as an aim in teaching controversial value issues see my 'The nature of understanding' in Hamingson, D. (ed) (1973). This is a discussion document intended for use by teachers engaged in the Humanities Project. The book as a whole contains a variety of papers and reports on the Project in schools including teachers' and pupils' reactions to the teaching role, and materials.

4

Understanding Others' Societies*

DAVID BRIDGES

Introduction

There is more or less an infinite number of things we *might* know about
another society or about societies in general; and whatever we do succeed
in knowing or understanding about a society, a nation, a community or
the way of life of a people, there will remain a massive number of other
things still to be known. (Henceforward, for simplicity's sake, I shall discuss
this problem in terms of understanding a *society*. A society is not, I know, the
same as a nation or a community, etc., but the differences are not material
to the issues raised in this discussion.) If we cannot hope to know *all* that
may be known about a society, is it possible perhaps to pick out certain
things as being *central* to gaining an understanding of it, as being more
important than others? For example, perhaps we could say that a knowledge of Marxist/Leninist teaching was crucial to an understanding of
Soviet Russian society today, while a knowledge of the achievements of
Soviet mountaineers was of only marginal significance. But on what
principle could we establish such priorities? How can we decide what is
crucial to an understanding of a society and what is less so? I want to sketch
three possible approaches to this problem: the first is based on a view of
the structure of knowledge; the second on a view of what a society *is*;
and the third on a view of certain key concepts which are basic and de-
limiting features of any human society.

SECTION 2
Understanding based on the structure of knowledge

There is no single unified form of enquiry which is the study of society.
Up to a point, therefore, the answer to the question 'what is central to an
understanding of a society?' will take a number of different forms. The
historian, the economist, the geologist, the anthropologist, the political

---

*This Chapter is probably best read in relation to Chapter 7 from which it was
  originally derived.

scientist and others will be likely to give different answers, for they will all be conducting their examination of society within their own frameworks of understanding, each one distinguishable here and there in terms of concepts employed, the kind of enquiry which is pursued or the type of explanation which is given.

Nor is it possible to escape interpreting a society from one, some or all of these points of view. These are the sort of ways man has evolved of making sense of his world (see Hirst, 1965,—though I am not following his precise divisions here). They are bound up in the language a man learns; and he ignores them at the price of intellectual anarchy and confusion. The man who wishes to understand society must do so under the aspect of the meaningful types of explanation contained within certain structured frameworks of knowledge.

The possibility of distinguishing these types of enquiry appears at first to complicate a decision as to what is of central importance in understanding a society, but it does in fact provide us with a basis for ordering and establishing some priorities. The structure of each form of enquiry of the kind that I have listed is related to an established view of the types of question it is worth asking and the kind of information which is relevant to an answer. In so far as I come to examine a society *qua* historian or *qua* anthropologist therefore, I will necessarily have a view, drawn from the tradition of my discipline, of what is important to an understanding of a society and what of peripheral significance. The historian, the physiologist or the anthropologist is bound by the nature of his enquiry to attach more importance to questions of one kind rather than another, to attend to certain sorts of evidence and certain kinds of explanation.

One response, then, to the question 'what is central to understanding a society?' is 'it depends what sort of enquiry you are engaged in'. Once we are clear about the kind of enquiry which is being pursued we can derive certain priorities from our understanding of the nature of that form of enquiry.

SECTION 3

Understanding based on what a society is

There is, however, an approach which may allow us to go further than this in getting to grips with what is involved in understanding a society. The general point can be made in this way: 'any view of what it is to understand an x (a work of art, a person, a society or anything else) depends upon a view of what an x *is*.' More specifically, one way of deciding what is central to an understanding of a society is to decide what it is that characterizes something as a 'society'. Let me illustrate this logical point in the context of 'understanding a work of art' and 'understanding a person' before developing the argument in relation to 'understanding a society'.

A man faced with a block of stone may offer a chemical analysis of its composition, a geological description of its history, an account of its size, weight and mass, or of its significance in a religious ritual; but all these insights would be of relatively peripheral significance if the object was presented to him as 'a work of art'. In this case the centrality of aesthetic concepts and judgements to an understanding of the object is indicated, indeed it is required, by the description under which the object is identified.

Similarly, it makes a crucial difference to what would count as understanding 'that creature over there' whether we conceived of it as a person, a naked ape or a sophisticated computer. Quite different kinds of description and explanation of its activities would be required according to our own conception of what it was. In so far as we regarded 'that creature over there' as a person (and a 'person' as, let us say, an agent having intentions and reasons, a centre of rights and duties) then clearly we would already be obliged, if we were consistent, to hold a particular view of the sorts of enquiry which would be central to an understanding of that creature—a view which would be radically different from one which stemmed from a conception of that creature in terms of, say, a stimulus response mechanism, caused behaviour and nothing more.

The view that we take of what is central to an understanding of a 'society' is even more governed by this sort of consideration. We can point at the block of stone, if not at the 'work of art'; we can point at the black, brown, yellow, or pinky-white creature, if not at the person; but not even this degree of ostensive definition is possible where society is concerned. A society is not locatable in time and space. It is not simply a number of people living in proximity to each other. To call a collection of people a society is to say nothing about their physical relationship at all. The members of the Jesuit priestly order are scattered about the world and through the ages, yet it is legitimate to regard them as a society in more than the narrow sense of a kind of 'club'.

I do not want to argue at length on a point which is not crucial to my main discussion, but it would be my claim that the main feature of any group of people we might call a society would be their common recognition of what can be called, in the broadest sense of the words, a shared system of rules or conventions. This system would commonly reflect shared values—but a system of shared values is neither a necessary nor a sufficient condition for a society. A society which is 'at war with itself', which does not enjoy a broad level of agreement at the level of basic values, may be an uncomfortable one to live in and it may not survive very long—but it may still be a society. A group of people, who happen to share certain values do not *eo ipso* become a society. In any case the notion of society involves something slightly more institutional, more operational. Let us suppose, then, that a society can be conceived of as a group of people having common recognition of some shared system of rules or conventions. This view, like any other, clearly has important implications for the decision as to what is central to an understanding of a society—as to what is to be understood above all else—and hence as to the kind of enquiry which is most relevant. It implies, in particular, that we cannot properly understand what is going on in a society without knowing something about the ways in which its members see *themselves* as operating. Peter Winch argues that 'the social relations between men and the ideas which men's actions embody are really the same thing considered from different points of view'. (Winch, 1958, p. 121.) Mine is the related but more extended claim that a society is only properly to be understood in terms of these ideas, and these ideas in turn, in terms of the rules, conventions or key concepts—some notions like compassion and dharma seem to me to be all three—of that society. This is because it is precisely these rules and conventions which transform what might otherwise be described as the behaviour of a collection of beings into what is properly called the activity of a society. How then can we know about the rules, conventions or key concepts under which people see themselves as acting? What sort of enquiry is required here?

The implication of my account is that the kind of enquiry conducted by the natural or even the social scientist, while making available interesting insights into human behaviour, cannot in principle offer what is central to an understanding of a society. For though these sciences may properly claim to observe regularities in the behaviour of persons, it will not be possible without knowledge of a different kind to judge whether these regularities are governed by rules or casually determined. On the view I have set out it is only the first of these which is centrally important to understanding a society.

On this view, understanding a society has in the end to depend on understanding the symbolic utterances of persons, for it is through their symbolic utterances, most notably and importantly in language, but also in the non-discursive use of signs and symbols, that people indicate the way they see things, the view they have of what they are doing, the patterns of conventions and rules under which they are acting.

That we need to know (and understand?) the rules, conventions, concepts, etc., under which a group of people see themselves acting, that we need perhaps even 'to see the world as others see it' in order to understand another society, presents us of course with a considerable challenge, not least where the society in question is a 'primitive' society in which the

whole framework of understanding, explanation and description of human
behaviour is different from our own (c.f. Winch, 1964, Hollis, 1968, and
references in each on the particular problem of understanding a primitive
society). In the face of this challenge we may very well fail to understand
a society or we may very well arrive at *an* understanding which is nonetheless a *mistaken* understanding of a society, where for example we describe
and explain the activities of a group of people in terms of rules, conventions and concepts which are themselves thoroughly consistent and
coherent but do not correspond with the view that the people themselves
have of their activities.

However, if the criteria for understanding a society turn out on this
analysis to be criteria which are difficult to satisfy, this is not a reason for
abandoning them. It may well be a difficult enterprise: understanding
people often is.

What I am suggesting, then, is that central to an understanding of a
society is knowledge about the rules and conventions which its members
accept commonly as a basis for the ordering and description of their
activities.

This is the more ambitious thesis here; my more general argument, to
which I should like to return, is, I think, an easier one to press. Even if my
accounts of the nature of a society and what follows from it as to what is
involved in understanding a society are mistaken, the procedural point
remains: *some* view of what a society is has to underlie *any* judgement about
what is central to understanding a society. If such a view is not arrived at by
careful thought and argument, it will nonetheless pervade every aspect of
any explanation, description or analysis which is entertained.

If a view of what in general a society is is thus so central to any understanding of a particular society, whence it is to be acquired? Not from any
empirical or *a posteriori* enquiry, certainly; for how would one know what
to investigate? Thus only by *a priori* reasoning, by the elaboration in fact
of a metaphysics of man singular and plural. We begin to see, in this
conclusion, the point of Winch's claim in *The Idea of a Social Science and its
Relation to Philosophy* that 'any worthwhile study of society must be
philosophical in character'. (Winch, 1958, p. 3). I am not very happy about
the total generality of this claim but I hope to have shown at least one area
in which it can be plausibly maintained.

SECTION 4
Understanding based on key concepts

In this third and last approach to the question of what is of central importance
to an understanding of society, I want to mention expositions from two

rather different sources of what I believe are in fact very similar arguments.

James Henderson, first of all, writes about what he calls 'constants and variables in human behaviour', an understanding of which he sees as one of the educational foundations of a happier world order. 'At all times and in all places', he says, 'just because of his human as distinct from his animal nature, man has required the satisfaction of certain basic needs, especially during the prolonged period of his infant and adolescent dependence on others: these can be summed up as the need to be fed, clothed, housed, loved, to love, to play and to work. These have been common to the twenty-odd civilizations of history as well as to the numerous more elementary societies. On the other hand, the manner in which these needs have been expressed and met are infinitely variable.' (Henderson, 1968, p. 9.)

Henderson is in fact concerned to do much more than explain what is involved in understanding a society, but his analysis does carry with it the thesis that central to such an understanding would be knowledge about the form taken in a society by the 'constants' of human experience.

This is a view not unlike that set out by Peter Winch towards the end of his article on 'Understanding a Primitive Society'. Winch tries to pick out what he calls the 'uniting concepts' of human experience—notions like birth and death, masculinity and femininity. He seeks to indicate how 'forms of these uniting concepts will necessarily be an important feature of any human society and that conceptions of good and evil in human life will necessarily be connected with such concepts. In any attempt to understand the life of another society, therefore, an investigation of the forms taken by such concepts and their role in the life of the society must always take a central place and provide a basis on which understanding may be built'. (Winch, 1964, p. 324.)

Put together, these statements suggest that there might be certain concepts (it is a further question what precisely these are) which will be and must be part of the framework of thinking of people of all societies—'must be' because they are bound up with experience which has inevitably been forced upon the attention of all people at all times. Such concepts, we might argue, would be of central importance in understanding any society, first because they are fundamental to man's experience—they define the limits within which the variable of human experience may be articulated; and secondly because they are *universal*—all men will share in some form of them, and the members of a particular society will necessarily share in one form of them. Indeed, it may very well be the fact of the universality of these key concepts, that is, the fact that there are certain constants in human experience, which affords the possibility of inter-societal understanding at all.

Summary

SECTION 1
This chapter began by asking what might be held to be central to an understanding of another's society.

SECTION 2
It was suggested that there was no single answer to that question; it depended very much on the kind of enquiry one was engaged in. It was possible however to claim certain kinds of knowledge (or understanding) as priorities, central to an understanding of a society.

SECTION 3
It was argued that these priorities might include *a priori* knowledge of the nature of societies in general and hence of the kinds of enquiry appropriate to their explication and, on a certain view of the nature of society, knowledge of the rules and conventions under which members of the society saw themselves as acting. This meant, in practice, understanding their symbolic utterances.

SECTION 4
A further approach to the understanding of other societies was through knowledge of the form taken in those societies of the 'limiting concepts' or 'constants' of human experience.

The chapter has not offered anything like a conclusive argument for the priority of these items but will, I hope, have offered sufficient argument for the conclusion to be examined seriously.

Further Reading

SECTION 2
The idea of logically distinct forms of knowledge or ways of structuring experience referred to in this section is developed by Hirst (1965). Phenix (1958) describes the structure of knowledge in comparable but interestingly different terms.

SECTION 3
Perhaps the most relevant sources to pursue in relation to this section would be those referred to in this essay—notably Winch (1958 and 1964) and Hollis (1968). It was Winch who claimed that 'any worthwhile study of a

society must be philosophical in character'. A contrasting case, for the *scientific* study of man, individual and social, is contained in Ayer (1967) and Gibson (1960).

SECTION 4
The ideas discussed in this section may be best followed up in Henderson (1968) and Winch (1965).

5

The Language of Social Education
PETER SCRIMSHAW

Introduction

The remarks that follow are basically concerned with two questions: what is involved in social education, and what contribution can different subjects make towards it?

I suggest that the fundamental component in social education is the development of social understanding, the quality and nature of which depends upon the extent, structural complexity and clarity of the language through which the pupils gain and express such an understanding.

I identify two possible sources from which this language might be drawn; the non-specialist vocabulary of the educated man, referred to as 'ordinary language', and the specialized terminologies of the social sciences.

Within the various school subjects which could be involved in social education I make a broad distinction between those (called here the humanities) which draw almost exclusively upon ordinary language, and those (labelled as the social science group) which involve, at least in part, the use of specialized language.

The claims of each approach that it alone can provide a totally adequate social education are then considered in turn, and finally rejected in favour of an approach which includes elements from both.

'Social Education'

In considering what is involved in social education a possible first response might be to wonder what it is not. Taken in its widest sense, social education could amount to all education, for in some respects all that we learn has social dimensions, is affected by the society in which we live, and affects in turn the contributions we are able to make to it.

However, it is in a much more restricted (and somewhat artificially delimited) sense that social education is to be considered in what follows.

The first restriction is one of content. I will assume that, in this narrower sense, a socially educated person is characterized by the possession of a sound and detailed understanding of himself and others, and also by his ability to behave in an intelligent and sensitive way in relation to others. This distinctly question-begging formulation will be developed more extensively below.

The second restriction relates to the method by which, and context within which, such social education may be gained. There is a great deal of evidence to show the important influence of the home, peer groups and other informal agencies upon the child's social development. Further, even if we restrict our consideration to the effects that teachers alone have here, much of this depends upon informal and individual contacts with children both outside and during lessons. In this informal setting, all teachers may affect the social development of the children they teach, at times when they have no intention of teaching them at all. But while all of these contexts are (or can be) important learning situations, I wish to consider only what might be called the consciously 'timetabled' element of such education, for this element is not without significance in its own right.

In this limited sense, 'social education' certainly picks out something that most schools and many teachers consider to be a definite part of their formal responsibilities. Within the context of secondary teaching, for example, teachers of history, social sciences, social studies, economics and moral education are all arguably concerned primarily with social education, while their colleague in the English, religious education and geography departments might all be plausibly expected to define social education as a *part* of their work.

It is precisely this diffusion of the work across many departmental boundaries that makes it important to attempt to get a clearer characterization of what it is that all concerned see themselves as collectively engaged in, if, that is, we accept that social education is important enough to justify serious and systematic thought and cooperation between the various teachers involved in it.

The socially educated person must possess an interrelated set of capacities, all of which must be developed up to a certain minimum level. To start with, he must be able to employ an extensive social vocabulary in a coherent and sensitive way, if his perceptions of himself and others are to extend beyond a set of crude stereotypes, dominated by the very specific cultural context within which he has grown up. His understanding of this vocabulary, however, must not be merely verbal. A sensitive and coherent employment of it means, on the contrary, that it is firmly related to the human behaviour that he observes. Moreover, it is nonsense to assume that somehow the mere addition of terms to such a vocabulary will automatically generate an increasingly differentiated pattern of perceptions. To some extent the individual must already feel the inadequacy of his current vocabulary in the face of the distinctions he perceives. However, if these perceived distinctions are to be registered permanently and made the object of further reflection, then new verbal distinctions will have to be learned to achieve this. The process is best seen as one in which perception, vocabulary and reflection all extend and differentiate each other in a complex cycle of mutual interaction.

At base, such a process must begin with what is immediately perceived, but any large degree of descriptive and explanatory sophistication will necessitate the inclusion of theoretical, abstract, or general terms whose relationship to what is observed is indirect. Such terms gain their meaning from their relationship to more basic ones. Thus, while such phrases as 'the French Revolution', 'middle class values' and 'authority' must, in the end, be rooted in the world as the pupil perceives it, they are only so rooted through their links with a variety of other, more concrete expressions.

While the possession of a social vocabulary is basic to social understanding, it is not all that such understanding involves. Such a vocabulary enables the pupil to formulate beliefs but he must also have some conception of the considerable variety of ways in which the appropriateness of these beliefs, and their relevance to decision making, can be at least roughly evaluated, if not decisively established. This is no simple matter. Consider, for example, how some historical knowledge, a sociological theory, a religious belief, and a memory of some personal experience might all play a part in our consideration of a really serious moral dilemma. All could be genuinely relevant to the problem in hand, but the way in which we try to establish and balance their very different sorts of importance is highly complex.

This leads to what is frequently seen as a third component in social education, namely the consideration of value issues of a social, political and/or moral nature. On the whole I personally find it hard to justify any rigid distinction between factual and theoretical components of social understanding on the one hand, and evaluative ones on the other. Whether such a distinction should be made is itself highly controversial, but even if it is to be made, then we must certainly include consideration of value issues within the broad context of social education as a whole. A conception of social education which assumes that the pupil should be encouraged to see his role in relation to others as that of an intelligently verbose spectator is, to say the least of it, incomplete.

But even including the consideration of value issues within the area of social understanding does not provide a complete account of social education. The pupil must not only be able to understand social situations correctly and evaluate possible courses of action in relation to them. He must also possess the skills and personal qualities that will enable him to translate his decisions into practice. It is, after all, one thing to recognize what ought to be done, another thing to bring yourself to attempt it, and another thing again to attempt it successfully. Taken together, these components constitute what might be meant by social education, where the content involved is conceived in the more limited way suggested earlier. What is still left in some doubt is how far all these components should figure in the formal part of a school's social education programme.

Clearly a sound social vocabulary is basic, but if this is to be employed with any real understanding, methods of judging the appropriateness of various sorts of social beliefs must also be to some extent grasped by the pupil. Therefore these two components must be given first priority. Insofar as moral evaluations are integral to this (as I believe them to be) they must be dealt with too. However, this must be done in a way which, as far as possible, avoids committing the pupil (through ignorance of other possibilities or an unreflective hostility to them) to specific moral positions. This can best be achieved by ensuring the widest possible range of alternative vocabularies within which moral and social choices can be formulated, and by methods of teaching which do not effectively exclude serious reflection about major alternative moral views of the world.

The development of social skills and qualities of character I would put last in the list of priorities for several reasons. First, the development of such capacities without the prior or simultaneous development of social understanding, could degenerate into a programme which at best taught pupils how to win friends and manipulate opponents, without giving them any yardstick by which to choose either, and at worst produced pupils who could not distinguish between acting morally and behaving correctly.

Secondly, while pupils can (and indeed inevitably do) practice social skills for themselves informally in schools, and later life, many of them may well never again have an opportunity to extend their social understanding and awareness in the company of others (both teachers and pupils) who are not of their own choosing. This would be a factor of some educational importance in a programme designed to broaden the social perspectives of those engaged in it.

Finally, there are various practical questions of time and resources to consider—and those in general seem to me to favour concentration upon the first three elements of social education rather than the last.

If this pattern of priorities is correct, then clearly the development of the pupil's understanding of what we might call 'social language' is of crucial importance. In addition we are faced with the problem of proposing some sort of reasonable division of labour amongst the wide range of subject specialists who could claim to have a distinctive contribution to make in this area. As we shall see, these two problems are interrelated.

SECTION 3
The Language of Social Education

If we look at language as a whole it is clear that it is by no means homogenous. Even leaving aside the complexities created by the existence of foreign languages, we can see that to understand English fully is not only to understand what might be vaguely described as 'ordinary language'. It also involves understanding a large number of more specialized vocabularies, related to ordinary language and to each other in complex ways.

This broad pattern is repeated within the more restricted area of social language. Here too we can discern ordinary language terms such as 'emotion', 'action', 'friendship' and 'responsibility', as well as more clearly specialized terms drawn from the technical vocabularies of, say, sociology or psychology. The expressions 'social mobility', 'negative effect' and 'I.Q.' would be examples of such specialized terms.

This distinction between ordinary and specialist language is central in what follows, and I hope what it involves will emerge more clearly later. But it is important at this stage to make clear that 'ordinary language' in this sense is not equivalent to the language used by the average man. Perhaps the sense required can best be expressed by identifying it as that language which we might reasonably expect any well educated person, whatever his specialist interests, to understand. This is inevitably vague, but will perhaps serve its purpose.

Defined in this way, ordinary language extends beyond the language of the ordinary (i.e. average) adult, although it must include this, for the language of the average man contains the basic framework of linguistic distinctions that characterizes ordinary language. What it lacks is the full range of vocabulary and semantic complexity present in the more fully developed version we have labelled 'ordinary'.

There remain two additional questions. The first is that of the relationship between the specialist language used in the technical vocabularies of, say, psychologists, and ordinary language. The second is how both are related to the sorts of language used in the various school subjects relevant to social education.

These relationships will be looked at in more detail below, but essentially I want to suggest that in selecting which of these subjects to teach we make one or other of two basic assumptions about the degree to which ordinary language can adequately express what we know about the relationships between ourselves and others.

The first of these views is embodied typically in the way we teach the social education component of subjects such as history, English literature and moral education, while some approaches to religious education and geography also exemplify it. Let us label this group of subjects, when approached in this way, as the humanities.

In these areas the basic assumption is that ordinary language, the natural mode of speech of well educated men, is a fundamentally adequate medium through which social understanding may be developed. It already embodies all the distinctions that are worth making, and provided the pupil comes to grasp the full complexity and subtlety of them, he will be fully equipped to understand the social aspects of his experience. This assumption directs the attention of both teacher and pupil towards those distinctions which have stood the test of time. In this respect the approach is fundamentally conservative (in a cultural, but not necessarily a political sense).

By contrast, the second group of subjects is marked by a reformative and innovatory approach to ordinary language. At the risk of some confusion, I will label these subjects the social sciences group. It includes not only economics, psychology and sociology, but also those approaches to geography, moral education and religious education that are characterized by the use of technical terms and a concern for explicitness and structure in the accounts they give of social experience. Notice that this is a significantly wider group than that normally referred to as the social sciences, and includes approaches to evaluative as well as descriptive and explanatory aspects of social understanding.

Within this group, the value of the conventional distinctions embodied in 'how we all speak' is, at best, provisional. The ultimate objective is seen as the replacement of the pupil's muddled, vague and cumbersome pattern of ordinary social language by one which is far more precise and effective, as an essential preliminary to the development of an exact and detailed form of social understanding. The humanities teacher sees the specialized vocabularies of the social sciences as unnecessary jargon. However, the social science specialist sees these vocabularies as the intellectual growth point in the whole area of social language, representing the initial stages in a linguistic transformation which must in the longer term fundamentally affect the clarity and accuracy of our conception of man.

At this point an obvious dilemma emerges. For if these two groups of subjects are based on such clearly contradictory assumptions then we seem to be forced to decide between the two. Either the study of the humanities is a laborious induction into an incoherent and muddled inheritance of past social misconceptions, or it is the only way by which a real feeling for the complexity of social experience can be gained. Conversely, either the social science subjects represent the only real way of cutting through the surface confusions to get a grip upon the underlying patterns of human behaviour, or they can be dismissed as complicated ways of making the obvious sound surprising and the ridiculous sound plausible.

However, these rather bleak alternatives are only forced upon us if we accept that the distinctions between the two types of language, and hence the distinction between the types of understanding they make possible, are really as mutually antagonistic as has been suggested. If they are not, then a justifiable balance (not to be confused with an expedient staffroom compromise) between them might be possible. To see if this is a possibility, let us look in turn at the claims made on behalf of the two contending approaches.

SECTION 4
The Case for the Humanities

Whatever else is to be said of the social segment of the ordinary language of educated men it is certainly not sparce in vocabulary or simple in structure. But to point this out is not the same as to accept the assertion that the vocabulary is repetitive or the structure an over-complicated muddle. On the contrary, detailed analyses carried out by philosophers during the last twenty years or so indicate that even two terms that seem at first sight to be identical in meaning are found, on closer inspection, to differ significantly. Further, within any set of related terms (say, for example, those referring to emotions or feelings) we can distinguish a complex and subtle pattern of interrelations of meaning.

While the reader must turn to actual analyses for detailed examples a quick illustration here might clarify the point. If, say, we take the word 'interesting', it might at first sight seem that it would serve to replace a number of other terms that have the same meaning. If we were concerned only to get a *rough* idea of what was going on when a person finds a situation interesting, then this would be true. But consider the range of further information which we gain when the situation is described as 'interesting in the sense of . . .

> strange, surprising, unexpected
> puzzling, confusing, informative,
> illuminating, revealing,
> useful, helpful,
> fascinating, intriguing.

Each of these groups of very rough equivalents for 'interesting' provide a more detailed (and a different) characterization of the way in which our interest is related to the overall situation. The last two groups, for example, distinguish something seen as interesting because of its relevance to some problem or plan the person is already considering, as against an interest purely in the thing itself. Now such distinctions can be of practical importance (as when a teacher needs to be able to tell if the children find what he says interesting/illuminating or just interesting/strange) and any psychological account of interest could be reasonably criticized as simplistic if its vocabulary was too limited to register such distinctions.

But while such groups of related terms in ordinary language are generally characterized by coherent patterns of internal relationships, the way in which such groups are related to each other is less clear cut. At present analytical philosophers are in the position of men who can describe the sequence of house street by street, but are confronted by continual puzzles and contradictions when they attempt to draw up a complete plan of the city. The reasons for this are themselves a matter of considerable doubt, but the fact remains that it cannot be asserted with any real confidence that, in total, ordinary language forms a consistent unit.

On the whole it seems far more likely that a number of alternative (and mutually exclusive) patterns of linkage could be partially justified be reference to the ordinary use of language, but no one pattern emerges which is both a descriptively accurate account of all such usage, and also free of internal inconsistencies. This is pretty much what one would expect to find within a society which contained a number of different world views and systems of values.

SECTION 5
The Case for the Humanities: a modified version

What has so far been pointed out is that ordinary language can, if properly used and understood, provide a much more subtle and well structured social language than its critics have suggested, and thus a more subtle form of social understanding as well. This claim is, however, limited by the recognition that there is no evidence to suggest that this internal coherence and pattern is so extensive as to suggest that ordinary language provides a unified and unambiguous medium through which social understanding may be developed.

Again, while it is more adequate than it seems, it remains an open question whether, even in terms of vocabulary alone, ordinary language is sufficient to express and record the modern complexities of social experience. It is at least possible that to achieve this, ordinary language must be supplemented by terms drawn from the technical expressions used in the social sciences.

The plausibility of this claim is partly masked by the tendency for specialized terms, once accepted, to become 'naturalized', merging over a period into the general body of ordinary language. Thus an expression such as 'inferiority complex' has now become part of the natural language of educated people, its technical origins being largely forgotten. In consequence, the defender of ordinary language against the incursions of technical terminology is in practice opposed only to the more recent newcomers. This is not as unreasonable as it appears if we accept the principle that in general new terms should be resisted until they have demonstrated their long term significance by successfully surviving such initial hostility; this would not be a policy of total linguistic conservatism, so much as one of linguistic caution.

On the other hand, the process of naturalization is at best a slow one, and involves in many cases a transformation of the meaning of the term involved which destroys much of its original precision and significance. If this is so, then it could be argued that the schools should actively promote linguistic innovation in certain areas by systematically extending the teaching of social science subjects to increasingly large numbers of pupils.

This would certainly be justified if we could identify any areas of social language in which neither the stock of ordinary terms, nor the gradual naturalization of well established technical terms were adequate to their tasks of description, explanation or evaluation. That such areas might exist is very plausible, for our language reflects what we notice about the world, which is invariably less than what there is to *be* noticed. In this sense, there is always room for further discriminations to be made, and for new terms to identify them.

But that alone is not enough. To discriminate endlessly just for its own sake is hardly practical. What must be shown is not only that new distinctions can be drawn, but that there would be some gain in doing so. Where this could be shown to be the case then, the introduction of the language of the social sciences would be clearly justified. But, as we saw in Section 2, merely to transplant the odd term or two will get us nowhere; such terms can only lead to understanding if they are seen within the context that gives them meaning. So to the extent that we need to teach certain terms from the social sciences, we are inevitably committed to teaching also the linguistic and methodological context which gives them their significance.

This involves reformulating our problem: are there any topics or problems within social experience that cannot be adequately dealt with using the language and methods of the humanities? If there are, then which of the vocabularies and approaches of the social sciences can deal with them most effectively? I believe that a considerable number of such topics could be identified; but let us look only at three examples which will illustrate the sort of possibilities that need to be considered.

The first lies within the sphere of social psychology; namely the systematic descriptive study of the processes by which individuals can influence the shape and direction of discussion and particularly decision-making procedures. I assume that at least in public there would be wide agreement that it is important for all pupils to recognize, for example, the distinctions between shared decision-making, consultation, and manipulation. While such distinctions must have been present in human discussion throughout historical time, difficulties of gaining access to, and accurate recording of, this kind of social interaction have tended to exclude descriptions of it from most historical writings. Again, while English literature contains such accounts, they tend to be fragmentary and indirect, leaving the nature of the processes involved only implicit in the account. No doubt this is partly because writers themselves may not have been fully conscious of the nature of the process they were attempting to recreate. Or perhaps in general it is rare for a writer's artistic intentions to lead him towards giving explicit accounts of such things.

Whatever the reason, my impression is that the humanities have largely failed to provide precise and detailed accounts of the ways in which such group activities are structured, altered and maintained, a failure which is partly a result of, and partly the reason for, inadequacies in the vocabulary of ordinary language at this point. In consequence, this is one area where social understanding is best gained through the sort of systematic and methodologically explicit investigation that characterizes good psychological enquiry.

A second topic might be the sort of organized study of moral problems that, in its most formal dress, would be labelled as ethics. The structural ambiguities noted earlier in ordinary language are at their most obvious in the sphere of morals, and such ambiguities are illustrated rather than resolved by the sorts of accounts which the humanities subjects provide. In a society where problems of moral explanation and justification are likely to become increasingly frequent, an opportunity for systematic and reflective discussion of them must have a preeminent claim to a place in the educational experience of all pupils. If it were agreed that a place should be found for such questions, then it would be probable that competence in the use of some of the specialist terms and methods used in philosophy and psychology would be distinctly valuable.

The third topic gives a particular importance to some aspects of sociology. The language of ordinary life originated in, and is still very largely adapted to deal with, problems and situations affecting only relatively small groups of people. In consequence it lacks an adequate vocabulary to describe and explain problems and activities which involve large numbers of people collectively engaged in complex institutions or activities. Fully to understand these aspects of social activity involves an acquaintance with sociological terminology, and some knowledge of the methods of enquiry employed. In particular, some grasp of the uses and limitations of elementary statistical techniques as aids to predicting social changes would be of obvious educational importance, provided it were intelligently presented within the context of a more general study of the methods of social research.

Further examples could easily be offered, but nevertheless the argument so far is in favour, in general, of a curriculum for social education in which the claims of the humanities would bulk large, even though time would be given to the social science approach, in areas where the humanities were manifestly unable to provide important sorts of social understanding.

Notice, though, that this position has been reached by showing only that the language of the humanities is not as inadequate as the most extreme supporter of the alternative group would argue. This would still leave a further counter argument that the devotee of the social sciences might advance.

SECTION 6
A Case for the Social Sciences

Such a devotee of the social sciences might concede that the humanities, with a certain amount of support from the social sciences, might well provide an adequate method of achieving the social education of the young; but this would still allow for the possibility of there being some alternative that was more than merely adequate.

Suppose there were a unified, independent and structurally superior language of the social sciences available as an alternative to ordinary language. It has been suggested that such a language would possess considerable advantages over ordinary language. In consequence those subjects which employed it would be educationally more effective than their rivals. Thus, rather than supplementing the humanities, the social sciences could justifiably replace them. But this assumes that such a language is already available, or at the very least, embryonically present in the specialized languages of our current social sciences; and this is a claim which must be investigated before it is accepted.

At its most extreme, the case for social education being conducted largely through the social science subjects rests upon a number of beliefs about the way in which the languages of these subjects (and consequently the sort of social understanding they can provide) differs from that of their competitors using ordinary language.

The central assumption is that ultimately ordinary language could, without significant loss, be replaced by an explicitly defined, clearly constructed unified language of the social sciences. Further, it is assumed that the ground plan for this language is already firmly laid in the technical language at present employed by social scientists. It is recognized, of course, that there are temporary confusions and overlaps within this language, but, it is suggested, the broad outlines are already sufficiently clear for it to be worth starting to replace the humanities by the social sciences as the educational medium through which social understanding is best achieved. But what are the advantages that could be claimed for the sort of understanding which the social sciences would provide? Again, these largely hinge upon claims made for the superiority of the language employed.

This superiority, it is suggested, has the following aspects. Within scientific language as a whole (and so within that part of it which relates to social experiences) the range of things which a term refers to is clearly delimited. This is often achieved by replacing the vague qualitative terms of ordinary language either by exactly quantitative ones, or by newly coined and clearly explained terms which are free of the vague associations that cluster around ordinary expressions. Further, the relations between the terms within this specialist language are clearly stated and consistently maintained by all those who use it. Thus, even where scientists use a term that also appears in ordinary language, its meaning within the specialist language is that embodied in its explicit definition; no more and no less.

Collectively these features provide a language marked by a high degree of clarity and consistency, in which the full meaning and referential range of the terms used is never in doubt. In consequence, the nature of assertions made using this language can be far more easily established. Similarly, descriptive claims are more easily checked than those made in ordinary language, and internal discrepancies or contradictions within an explanatory account are made more readily visible.

These features in turn make possible a clearer distinction between description, explanation and evaluation, while the final requirement (that the methods of investigation used must themselves be unambiguous and explicitly stated) completes the picture of a highly structured, rational and effective language.

Now it is certain that if we had such a unified language of the social sciences then the argument in favour of declaring the humanities redundant as agents for social education would be a strong one. However, as yet no such language, and consequently no such unified social science, is available. To point this out is not to join the ranks of those who think numeracy the mark of a vulgar mind, but it is to recognize that in our current stage of development this potentially unified science is embodied in a number of distinct or semi-distinct disciplines within the social sciences area, revealing (in methodology, subject matter and terminology) a confused pattern of interrelationships and incompatibilities.

Further, even within any one of these disciplines (say, sociology) the criteria which were earlier suggested for a systematized and independent scientific language remain commendable ideals rather than functioning realities. It is certainly true that such terms as 'middle class', 'family' and 'role' are far more likely to receive explicit definitions from a sociologist than from a layman, and such definitions go some way towards increasing the consistency and clarity of what is said in specialist as against ordinary language. However, the proportion of terms which are so defined in any piece of sociological (or psychological) writing is small. The remainder of the work, and indeed often the definitions themselves, employ ordinary language in what is (to all intents and purposes) an ordinary way. Again, it is probably true that social science writings are marked by a somewhat greater degree of explicitness and consistency of usage than ordinary writing; but this is a difference of degree, not a difference in kind.

In general, I do not believe that the case for the present existence of a scientific alternative to ordinary social language can be supported. What we do have here are a number of different disciplines, characterized in part by differences in technical terminologies, but all employing languages that are, to a greater or lesser extent, terminologically coextensive with ordinary language and not entirely different from it in clarity and explicitness.

However, this does not mean that the social science subjects cannot justifiably claim a place within the area of social education. On the contrary, as we have already seen, even on the view most favourable to the humanities, there are definitely areas in which an appeal to the social sciences is preferable or even unavoidable. Nor does that complete the argument in their favour. If the language they employ is not totally different from that of the humanities, neither is it totally the same. On the contrary, it emphasizes qualities of explicitness, clarity and simplicity that encourage an attitude towards the investigation of social experience that has a great deal to recommend it, and is distinctively different from that produced by the study of the humanities. Further, I believe that it is important that pupils have a sufficient opportunity to consider both the appropriateness of seeing human activity as a subject for explicit and systematic investigation, and also to discover the limitations and difficulties involved in any attempt to achieve this. Neither of these aims could be achieved without the pupil being substantially involved in some of the social sciences.

In summary then, if the arguments advanced in these remarks have substance, we are led to the somewhat unexciting (but perhaps useful) conclusion that neither the humanities or the social sciences alone can claim to provide an adequate approach to social education. Rather the curriculum must include substantial components from both, if sound social understanding is accepted as an important educational objective.

Further Reading

SECTION 2

A fuller discussion of the links between language, belief and action can be found in *Philosophy and Education*, chapter 5 (Langford, 1970), while some aspects of the relationship between perception and language are dealt with in *The Philosophy of Primary Education*, chapter 6 (Dearden, 1968).

SECTION 3

The general question of the relationship between ordinary and scientific language is taken further in *The Structure of Science*, chapter 1 (Nagel, 1961); in *Logic: the Theory of Inquiry*, part 1 (Dewey, 1938); and in *The Nature of Historical Explanation*, part 1 (Gardiner, 1952).

SECTION 4

Examples of the sort of analysis described here can be found in *The Concept of Mind* (Ryle, 1963) or *The Philosophy of Mind* (White, A. R., 1967).

An excellent discussion of the way in which terms may have different meanings in different historical periods, or within different systems of values, is included in *A Short History of Ethics* (MacIntyre, 1967).

SECTION 5

The sort of developments in social psychology discussed here are illustrated by *Working with Groups* (Klein, 1963), *The Psychology of Inter-personal Behaviour* (Argyle, 1967), or by many of the articles in *Social Psychology of Teaching* (Morrison and McIntyre, 1972). A particularly interesting book is Hargreaves, D. (1967). Apart from its practical value for teachers, it illustrates how literary sources and technical research results can be brought to bear on practical problems in social education. Some of the comments in the introduction are particularly relevant to the issue discussed above.

An illustration of how an understanding of the social sciences could assist in the pupil's moral education is provided in chapter 9 of *Introduction to Moral Education* (Wilson, Williams and Sugarman, 1967).

SECTION 6

For arguments largely supporting the independent status of scientific language, see particularly May Brodbeck's introduction to *Readings in the*

Philosophy of the Social Sciences (Brodbeck, 1968), and the chapter from Nagel's book already mentioned.

GENERAL

The reader might find it of interest to consider what has been said in relation to the work of the Schools Council Integrated Studies Project, the publications of the Farmington Trust on Moral Education (Wilson, Williams and Sugarman, 1967) and the materials and methods which have been generated by the Schools Council Humanities Project (see references in John Elliott's article). As an example of the way in which a subject within the humanities group might be geared, in part at least, towards social education, the reader is referred to *English for Maturity* (Holbrook, 1967), and *Sense and Sensitivity*, chapters 8 and 9 (Creber, 1965) in which the potential relevance of various aspects of English teaching to moral and social understanding are illustrated.

Finally, an energetic justification for the inclusion of what I have called social education in the curriculum is given in John Wilson's article *Two Types of Teaching* (Wilson, 1965).

6

Knowledge of Others and Concern for Others

CHARLES BAILEY

SECTION 1
Introduction

Much of education is concerned with helping pupils to improve their understanding of personal relationships and their understanding of what it is to know other people. In moral education, for example, we wish to increase pupils' concern for others, and to this end we try to develop pupils' awareness, understanding and knowledge of other people. Apart from moral education many schools concern themselves with work in which *the person* is of central importance, and in which relations between persons, and the ways in which persons understand and know one another, are the objects of study. This essay is not essentially about ways of achieving success in these areas of study, but rather about the nature of the understanding of others, the knowledge of others and the concern for others that we are trying to bring about. The analysis is conducted in the belief that no systematic education can possibly be undertaken unless we are reasonably clear about what it is we are trying to achieve.

In much recent literature about social and moral education knowledge of others and concern for others have often been discussed in terms of 'empathy' and 'sympathy'. It is proposed to argue in this essay that these two terms have brought more confusion than clarity into discussion about persons, and that they are better dispensed with. The confusion will be demonstrated by discussing some of the different senses in which 'empathy' and 'sympathy' are used. A short critical section will then lead to an account of knowing others and concern for others which seems possible without using terms like 'empathy' and 'sympathy'. The essay will conclude with a discussion of some implications of the argument for education about persons, particularly moral education.

SECTION 2
Empathy

The term 'empathy' did not enter our language until 1912 as a translation of the German *Einfuhlung*, or in-feeling, which means the power of projecting one's own personality into the object of contemplation and so understanding it. The object of contemplation in these early usages of the term was usually a work of art, but the usage was soon extended to the understanding of other people, and this seems to be the most common usage in recent literature. There are, however, at least five distinctively different meanings given to 'empathy' even when the term is used to refer to knowing or understanding other people. These five different senses may be named:

(i) 'empathy' a simple synonym for knowing or understanding others;
(ii) 'empathy' as motor mimicry;
(iii) 'empathy' as imagining myself in the place of others;
(iv) 'empathy' as evoking the other within myself;
(v) 'empathy' as a rather mysterious way of knowing that goes beyond any normal modes of cognition.

Little need be said about sense (i) except to note that although it might well be a convenient shorthand it conveys nothing more than the words 'knowing' or 'understanding' do. 'Empathizing' is simply 'knowing' when the object of knowing is a person.

Sense (ii), however, indicates a rather more specific way of knowing others. What is suggested is that when we watch other people in action, especially in some action like running or jumping, our own nervous and muscular system tends to mimic what is seen. Our own sensations arising from this mimicry give us the feelings that constitutes a knowledge of what the other is doing and feeling. Some writers have offered evidence of this mimicry in photographs of people watching athletes and imitating, sometimes in large numbers, the actions of the athletes. One such picture (see Allport, 1938, p. 530) shows an athlete passing horizontally over a high bar in a pole vault, having just let go of the pole. That the spectators are undergoing physical tension, as well as the athlete, is evident enough, but the manner in which they are showing it is hardly evidence of straight-forward non-reflective motor-mimicry. For, in fact, a number of them are lifting one leg off the ground in what looks like an incipient straddle or scissors jump, bearing little resemblance to the style of a pole-vault. This would seem to indicate a good deal of cognitive structuring, as though the spectators' mimicry was not of the athlete's *actual* motor activity, but rather of the spectators' *conception* of the activity, based on their own simpler notion of jumping.

Sense (iii) is common in literature about moral education. One writer, for example, describes a girl's response to a picture of a child drowning viewed by a lone onlooker on the bank: 'She thinks how she would feel if she were in the water'. (See Bull, 1969, p. 39.) Phrases like 'entering into the minds and hearts of other people', 'stepping into other people's shoes', or even 'How would *you* like to be treated like that?', or 'Suppose it happened to you?' are all invitations to imagine ourselves in the place occupied by someone else, to project ourselves, by imagination, into the place of another.

This sense of 'empathy' has been contrasted with sense (iv), which is markedly different. This is to evoke the other person within oneself. That is, not to imagine oneself in the other's place, but to imagine *being* the other. The difference is a most important one. What is often the most important thing to understand in someone else's problem is what it is like to be *that person* in those circumstances, not what it would be like to be *me* in those circumstances. All kinds of advice, including moral advice, is often prefixed by the formula: 'If I were you I would . . .' when, of course, the real difficulty arises from the fact that the person is *not* the adviser, but someone else, with different characteristics, temperament and capabilities. It would seem clear that any attempt to understand others must involve attempts to see things from *their* point of view, and that this does not mean their geographical point of view alone, but seeing things as they see them, with their conceptions, beliefs, attitudes and suppositions.

The fifth and last sense of 'empathy' I have picked out is that sense in which knowledge of others is gained by some process or relationship which goes beyond normal methods of knowing objects other than persons. Sometimes this seems to be a kind of sharing of feelings or emotions with the other person. Sometimes, however, what is emphasized is the relationship or communication one must have with another person to know that person. This sense of 'empathy' is contrasted with scientific or objective knowing, and is common in psychotherapeutic literature and in the work of writers about counselling and social welfare work.

We thus have usages of the word 'empathy' ranging from non-cognitive motor mimicry, through various kinds of cognitive and imaginative appraisal, to modes of knowing claimed to transcend the merely cognitive or intellectual by means of feeling or relational rapport. Except for the fact that all this is applied to knowing and understanding other people, these diverse usages seem hardly to constitute even a family resemblance.

SECTION 3
Sympathy

The term 'sympathy' has had a longer history in English than 'empathy'. It has always had the connotation of some kind of accord between two separate things, but in early usages these two things were not necessarily people. Two material or non-personal substances could be described as 'sympathetic' if they had certain characteristics or properties in common. This usage seems to have passed away and the word is used today in reference to fellow-feeling or accord between people. Nevertheless, there are again distinct differences in usage as important as those we have noticed in the case of 'empathy'. Again we may distinguish five important variations:

(i) 'sympathy' meaning straightforward accord or agreement;
(ii) 'sympathy' as a synonym for 'empathy' or knowing others;
(iii) 'sympathy' as fellow-feeling more or less innate;
(iv) 'sympathy' as fellow-feeling brought about by thought about the circumstances of the other;
(v) 'sympathy' as active, or involving active concern and compassion, love, agape, etc.

For the members of a committee to say that they are in sympathy about a proposal indicates nothing about concern for others, but merely that no one is going to argue further. This is the meaning of sense (i). People can agree, or 'sympathize' with one another in this sense, without having 'sympathy' for one another in any of the other senses to be mentioned.

We can be similarly brief about sense (ii). To 'sympathize' with someone in this sense is to know or understand their feelings, to realize that they are sad, miserable or whatever, but not necessarily either to share their feelings or to be concerned about them.

The third sense of 'sympathy', that it is innate fellow-feeling, has been very influential. Writers on moral education have seen sympathy in this sense as providing the basis of sociability, reciprocity and altruism. (See Bull, 1969, p. 97.) Sympathy thus becomes part of our moral concern for others, but is also offered as an explanation of this concern.

Such accounts remind us of the importance attached to the notion of sympathy by David Hume in his account of morality. (See Hume, 1969, p. 507.) Hume subscribed to, and developed, the idea that moral judgements derive not from reason but from approbation or otherwise of a moral sense, held to be innate and affective. Hume, however, embedded these notions in a careful and consistent connection with the notion of sympathy. Sympathy, for Hume, is the propensity we have to receive by communication the inclinations and sentiments of others, however different they may be from our own. This is brought about, first, by our observation of 'external signs in the countenance and conversation' which convey to us the idea of the inclination or sentiment. But our natural make-up is such that an idea of affection is likely to be lively enough to produce a similar affection in the observer, largely because the relationship between our affections and 'the internal operations of the mind' is so strong. (See Hume, 1969, pp. 366–374).

Hume's claim for sympathy is a particularly demanding one. We are not simply imagining ourselves in the situation of the other, we are entering directly into the affections of others. 'This is the nature and cause of sympathy', says Hume, 'and 'tis after this manner we enter so deep into the opinions and affections of others, whenever we discover them'. (Hume, 1969, p. 369.) Hume is thus sure that we have this direct contact with the affections of others, that this fires our own affections, and so enters directly into our sentiment of approval or otherwise of acts affecting the happiness and welfare of human beings. The moral sense is thus more than merely subjective, since it is steeped in a sympathetic communication with others which is part of the natural make-up of human beings.

Others, whilst noting the phenomenon of fellow-feeling, have given rather a different account of it. One example of such a different account is that given by Adam Smith, a contemporary of David Hume, in his *Theory of Moral Sentiment*. These eighteenth-century writers are of interest here because they pick out two views of sympathy which are continually used in modern writing on moral education. Adam Smith considered that an 'analogous emotion' appeared in the observer of someone else's emotion, but that this appeared not from the signs of the emotion, as Hume had said, but 'at the thought of the situation'. (See Smith, A., 1964.) There is good reason to support this view, since we clearly are influenced by the situations in which we see others, even sometimes when they themselves are not so affected: we feel sorry for the fool who does not feel sorry for himself; we feel embarrassed by the *faux pas* of our friend who feels no embarrassment himself; and we feel sad for the dead man who now feels nothing at all. These are all feelings consequent upon some cognitive appraisal of situations. In many cases this will lead to us having the same, or similar, feelings to those felt by the person we are observing, and we would rightly call this fellow-feeling or sympathy. It is noteworthy, however, that we would still talk of sympathy even in those cases where the feelings were not those of the person observed, but rather the feelings of the observer arising from his appraisal of the situations. This is much more like our fourth sense of 'sympathy', involving the imagining of oneself into the situation of the other.

There are obvious similarities between the two senses of 'sympathy' just described and the two senses of 'empathy' concerned with knowing or understanding others by either imagining oneself in their situations or imagining what it is like to *be* the other. The difference lies in the fact that 'empathy' in both cases names a *kind of knowing or understanding*, whilst 'sympathy' in both cases names a *type of fellow-feeling* accounted for in two different ways.

Jean Piaget, in his work on *The Moral Judgement of the Child*, acknowledged a kind of innate or instinctive sympathy when he wrote: 'the child's behaviour towards persons shows signs from the first of those sympathetic tendencies and effective reactions in which one can see the raw material of all subsequent moral behaviour'. Piaget, however, was quite clear that sympathy so described was not sufficient for morality. He also wrote: 'As for sympathy, it has of itself nothing moral in the eyes of conscience. To be sensitive alone is not to be good . . .' (See Piaget, 1932, p. 395.)

It is in recognition of the fact pointed out by Piaget that some modern writers on the nature of moral concern have used a stronger sense of 'sympathy' which is sometimes called 'active sympathy', and means something like 'the sympathy of practical concern for others as distinguished from simply feeling with them'. R. S. Downie and Elizabeth Telfer attach considerable importance to this usage of 'sympathy' in their influential book *Respect for Persons*. 'In so far as persons are thought of as self-determining agents who pursue objects of interest to themselves we respect them by showing active sympathy for them; in Kant's language, we make their ends our own. In so far as persons are thought of as rule-following we respect them by taking seriously the fact that rules by which they guide their conduct constitute reasons which may apply both to them and to ourselves. These two components are independently necessary and jointly sufficient to constitute the attitude of respect which is fitting to direct at persons, conceived as rational wills.' (See Downie and Telfer, 1969, pp. 28–9.)

This fifth sense of 'sympathy' as active concern clearly adds something to simple notions of fellow feeling, however the latter are explained or accounted for. Here we have actual concern, actual regard or respect for the other person. This is more like the Christian notion of agape or love, and merges into even stronger notions like compassion. To have actual concern for others is an element in morality in a way that the simple fact of fellow-feeling is not. Simply to feel the same as someone else is not necessarily to have concern *for* that someone else. Sensitivity, as Piaget says, is not enough. Downie and Telfer insist that active sympathy is natural and possessed to some extent by everyone. They argue, indeed, that it follows as a matter of fact, and possibly conceptually, from the more passive kinds of fellow-feeling which human beings are said to possess innately or instinctively.

SECTION 4
Criticism

Whatever their convenience in ordinary conversation, words are only useful in serious discussion if they name concepts which are reasonably clear and distinguishable from other concepts, and if the important distinctions and demarcations between some concepts and others are not more clearly indicated in other ways. What has already been shown about the terms 'empathy' and 'sympathy' is that they do not fulfil this useful function but instead introduce confusions rather than clarity into discussions of inter-personal life and inter-personal understanding. It is thus suggested that educators, counsellors and others concerned with these areas of understanding, will be better served by other ways of discussing the problems of concern for others and knowledge of others. The terms 'empathy' and 'sympathy' name not two concepts which are distinguishable one from another, but a multitude of concepts which are confused with one another by the use of these terms and therefore confuse issues and problems.

In particular, the terms appear to confuse and conflate distinctions that *are* important. For example, the different uses of 'sympathy' confuse the distinction between feeling or being in accord or having fellow-feeling with someone, on the one hand, with having respect or love or compassion for someone, on the other. When Christ tells us to love our enemies this only makes sense if two different senses of consideration of the other are involved. What we are being urged to do is to respect even those for whom we have no fellow-feeling, a perfectly sound moral injunction, but difficult to understand if love, or respect, is to be a strong sense of the sympathy or fellow-feeling which the term 'enemy' suggests we lack. The first of these actions, accord or fellow-feeling, is to do with the *sharing* of feelings, attitudes, dispositions or beliefs. The sharing of any *particular* feelings, attitudes, dispositions or beliefs might well be a highly contingent and coincidental matter, whereas there might be more general feelings, attitudes, dispositions or beliefs, the sharing of which is a less contingent matter, more characteristic of being a person. This, of course, would have to be shown, and I shall return to this in the next section of this essay.

The second notion, that which moves over the continuum of respect, love and compassion, is clearly concerned with more than sharing and more than fellow-feeling, since ideas like respect, love and compassion name the having of positive normative attitudes towards others. That there might be logical, conceptual or substantive connections between these two notions is a plausible hypothesis, a likely direction in which to think, but what exactly the connections are needs showing. To use the same word, 'sympathy', to name such distinctively different ideas, preempts and inhibits the necessary thought and confuses the outcome. In particular, confusion arises because the *description* of the phenomenon of fellow-feeling penetrates the justificatory problem presented by ideas like respect. You do not ask why you should have fellow-feeling, you have it or you do not; but you *do* ask why you should respect persons, because respect is the kind of notion of which it can be said that it ought to be present if it is lacking.

The same difficulties and similar confusions arise when the term 'empathy' is offered as being helpful to our discussions about understanding and knowing others. Important distinctions between ways of trying to understand others are confused by using the same term. For example, 'empathy' names both understanding others by imagining *myself* in their circumstances, and attempting to understand the same circumstances from the point of view of *the other*. In studies like history, literature and certain aspects of human geography, as well as in personal relationships and morality, this is a vitally important distinction to make. If I can never get nearer to understanding the actions of, say, Robespierre than imagining my twentieth-century self in his eighteenth-century shoes, my understanding is likely to be limited indeed. It also conveniently ignores the very real difficulties inherent in any attempt to see things as Robespierre saw them. This difficulty is only a special case of a general range of problems like trying to understand my wife, my child, my pupils or any of my fellow human beings. I cannot hope to understand them simply by putting myself into their shoes, or even into their roles.

We must, therefore, emphasize this important distinction and not blur it or conflate it. We need to examine the connection, if any, between these different ways of trying to make sense of other people's actions, and we can only do this by being clear that there *is* a difference. A common name is therefore a hindrance and an encumbrance.

The use of the term 'empathy' as some special mode of knowing or understanding which extends beyond normal methods of cognition presents another type of confusion. What we have in actuality is a problem of how we know about other minds, given that individual minds have an obvious privacy. In spite of the apparent difficulties, we *do* claim to know things about the motives, intentions, purposes and even the feelings of other people. To resolve this difficulty, the term 'empathy' is offered as the name of some special quality enabling knowledge of persons to take place in a way that involves either some kind of special insight attendant upon fellow-feeling or rapport, or some special mode of knowing depending on the personal relationship itself. Now simply using the term does nothing at all about solving the problem of knowing others. It simply covers up the difficulty by substituting other notions for knowledge, namely fellow-feeling, rapport or relationship, and another notion for the process of knowing, namely empathy. In fact, of course, there is no evidence that we have anything other than the normal methods of cognition and conceptualization to go on, though it is certainly the case that normal methods of cognition and conceptualization can be used with more or less skill in trying to understand others. Nevertheless, to posit some super-cognitive mode of understanding others is to foreclose on the genuine enquiry and replace it by a quasi-magical procedure called empathizing.

It seems, then, highly desirable to dispense with these terms which confuse important distinctions and offer labels instead of answers to serious problems, and to attempt some direct and positive account of understanding and respecting other people.

SECTION 5
An Alternative Account of Knowing and Respecting Others

The first important point in any coherent account of knowing and respecting others is that relating to persons, or understanding other persons, must involve conceiving of these others *as* persons. There is a whole community of discourse and action dependent upon the irreducibility of the notion of a person. By 'person' I mean a *rational living body*. There is a distinct change in our mode of apprehension and in the consequence of our conceptualizations when we see something as a living body compared with seeing something merely as a physical body. These differences are even more marked when we see something as a person—as a rational living body. The important distinctions seem to lie between conceptualization something like this:

(a) non-living bodies—things
(b) non-sentient living bodies—plants
(c) non-rational sentient living bodies—animals
(d) rational living bodies—persons

Physically, the borderlines between groups of phenomena conceptualized in these four ways are difficult to draw: some plant life seems sentient, some humans are non-rational, virus forms occupy a zone between living and non-living. But these examples do not alter the fact that we make these different conceptualizations, or the fact that we act and react according to the different conceptualizations we make. We bother about borderline cases because we want to know how to act before the presented phenomenon, we want to know how to treat it, and we will treat it according to our conceptualization of it.

I am arguing, then, that in certain frameworks of discourse and action, namely those to do with practical reason, the person or rational living body is a necessary and irreducable conception. Necessary, because without such a conception the framework of discourse and action cannot exist. Irreducible, because to try to enter these frameworks of discourse and understanding on the basis of considering parts of persons (organs, nerves, cells, molecules, stimuli and responses) is in fact to circumscribe oneself in a *different* framework of discourse and understanding. This different framework is probably scientific, and is certainly observational and spectatorial when the discourse and understanding connected with practical reason is about the human being as agent, mover or actor.

Part of being able to use this central and unifying concept of a person would be the knowledge of certain characteristics necessarily attributed to those recognized as persons. Recognition of something as a person involves the attributions to the other of feelings, capacities for pleasure and pain, intentions, reasons, purposes and autonomous choice that can be manifested in action, and *all* recognition of persons would involve such attributions. This is no argument from analogy with what I know of myself, for I have to learn that *I* am a person and what this involves, as well as coming to know that *others* are persons and what this involves. Rather it is an argument for the sense in which a framework of conceptions concerning considerations about what we ought to do can be made coherent.

Even simply to conceive of what presents itself to me as a person, then, means that I am conscious of this other as a rational living body, susceptible to pleasure and pain, capable of purposes and intentions, free choice and decision, an autonomous centre of consciousness and reason. In the normal case I recognize a person by rather obvious physical signs displayed by human beings—their shape and general physiological presentation. These signs do not *prove* the existence of all the attributes of a rational living being, but in the normal case they are taken as indicating the presence of these attributes. I do not seek proof of the existence of these attributes every time I meet a human being; rather I take them as given unless I am presented with reasons for suspecting their absence in the form of odd behaviour. On the other hand, if someone seeks to convince me that a non-human being, for instance a monkey, a machine or an angel, has the attributes of a person, then the onus is clearly on that someone to demonstrate that the attributes exist in these cases as well.

The judgement that something presents itself to me as a person is normally an all or nothing affair. My friend is a person and my armchair is not; my nephew is a person and my dog is not. Normally, we only have doubts about this in the case of children. A new-born babe is not a person in the sense used here. With help he becomes a person, and the fact that he *can* become a person is the reason for treating him with some of the respect normally shown to persons. To treat him with none of this respect would adversely affect his chances of becoming a person.

As well as recognizing these kinds of attributes in recognizing persons, it also follows that one must *respect* persons. There is, however, confusion about what this means. The argument sometimes runs as follows: the existence of certain attributes in those we recognize as persons constitutes a reason for having a valuing attitude named respect towards such persons. The trouble with this argument is that it commits the fallacy of passing from a statement of what *is* the case to a statement of a different kind, namely, a statement of what we *ought* to do. But respect for persons can be seen not as respecting or valuing *because* of certain attributes, but rather in a somewhat lower key where respect for persons means respecting persons *as having* certain attributes. To conceive of something as a person with all the attributes necessary to such a conception cannot involve treating that something as though *not* a person without inconsistency. Once something is conceived of *as* a person most of the respect is already granted; any subsequent action which does not treat the person as a person is unjustifiably inconsistent. To conceive of something as a person and to treat the person accordingly *is* to respect persons. Respect is not something added on to this for which additional reasons have to be sought. To treat someone as a rational living being is to respect them as persons. Respect for persons, so considered, would thus be a certain kind of conceptualization *and* action in accordance with that conceptualization. What would be a nonsensical claim, on this argument, would be that I could recognize someone as a person, treat him accordingly, that is treat him as one possessing the necessary attributes of a rational living being, and yet not respect him. A failure to respect a person, in this basic sense, is a failure to treat him as a possessor of the attributes of a rational living being. For example, to treat him as though incapable of rational choice, of acting on reasons, or as though he had no capacity for feeling or suffering, would be failure to respect him as a person.

There is, of course, a much more honorific sense of 'respect', as when I say I greatly respect Winston Churchill or Chairman Mao, where the intention is obviously comparative. Our basic sense, however, is both more general than this and of much greater importance in education and in inter-personal life.

Two objections might be made to this general analysis of respect for persons. One might argue: (*a*) why should I conceptualize human beings in this way? And (*b*) even if conceptualized in this way, what is to stop me deciding to treat people for some purposes as though not rational living beings?

The answer to the first objection is that it is necessary to conceive of human beings in this kind of way partly because they do have these characteristics or, in the case of young children, can be helped to develop them. It is also necessary, however, because the framework of concepts embodied in the language of inter-personal life could not work together in a coherent fashion without this central and categoreal concept. Not only the moral life, but all purposeful and justifiable activity, all agreements, discussions, blamings and praisings, urgings and persuadings, all practical decisions and reasoning about practical activities, all the most characteristic-ally human activities taken for granted even by the least moral and most selfish of us, would be pointless, or at least incoherent and inconsistent, without the concept of a rational living being at the heart of all the discourse and activity.

The answer to the second objection is simply that to treat persons as *not* rational living beings is to be inconsistent. This may be unimportant to some people, but they cannot *argue* that it is unimportant, for that, surely, would be to value both consistency *and* inconsistency at the same time. To argue at all is to accept the point of basic assumptions like consistency. To be concerned at all about what one ought to do is only intelligible as seeking reasons within a consistent framework of reasons.

A person who lives as though these objections did have force is the rational egoist: he is a person who tries to be rational on his own behalf but under no obligation to treat others as rational living bodies. There is little doubt that many people do try to operate under this maxim or something very much like it. The difficulty with this position is again that it cannot be maintained consistently unless the egoist is prepared to set himself up as a complete slave-master, with all other humans mere extended instruments of his will. To do this would be, first, to ignore the many evidences that others *do* operate as rational living bodies, and, secondly, to forgo the multitude of advantages and possibilities that come into being in terms of relationships with other rational living bodies, and in terms of the material and mental products of other beings acting as centres of rationality. In fact those people we see as rational egoists act anything but rationally, since they do not bother about the inconsistency in their view of other humans, accepting them for some purposes as rational living bodies but for other purposes conceiving of them in a more limited fashion.

In the area of concern for others and knowledge of others, then, it seems necessary to possess a certain conceptual framework. At the heart of this framework is the concept of a person—a rational living body. This makes possible a whole network of other concepts like intention, purpose, responsibility, praise and blame which collectively constitute moral dis-course, and, with the behaviour they characterize, the moral life itself. It is also argued that respect for persons, or basic concern for others, describes both the *recognition* of persons *and the treatment* of them as persons. In this sense it is like respecting a bone china cup by carrying it carefully, or respect-ing the fire by not standing too close to it; that is, we respect things and persons by treating them according to basic conceptions of what they are, according to attributes they necessarily embody if conceived as such.

These conceptions and actions in accordance with them would be necessary for the inter-personal life, or for a rational morality, but clearly are not sufficient. For although I am now provided with general reasons for treating my fellows as rational living beings, I am not provided with any applicable content about how to treat a particular rational living body in particular circumstances *as* a person. It is in these particular cases of which the moral and inter-personal life is compounded that the great diversity of the life of rational living bodies presents itself. Knowledge of this diversity, of its range and of specific examples of it, has to be acquired.

Such knowledge or experience is basically of two kinds, which might be distinguished as knowledge *about* others and knowledge *of* others. The first gives me a range of possibilities; the second gives me the specific knowledge of the other or the others with whom I am involved in any particular circumstance. In part, knowledge of the first kind is derived gradually but cumulatively from my direct experience of an increasing number of circumstances involving others. The immersion in the world of personal action and interaction is as persistent and pervasive as immersion in the world of language, and together these distinctively characterize the significant environment of human development. But knowledge of this first kind also comes from the experience of reading literature, seeing films and dramatic performances, studying history and generally being exposed to the range and variety of actual and imaginable human action. Out of all this I build up a stock of imaginable possibilities of human action, ways of conceiving of human action, ways of giving possible content to the formal notions of intentional action already presupposed in conceiving of some things as persons.

The knowledge of the second kind is that knowledge by which I place particular clues coming from another person or persons and locate the behaviour in my framework of possible behaviours. The knowledge by which I understand particular others in this way is what is sometimes called empathy, or explained as some special kind of cognition different from others. The argument of the present analysis is that knowledge is only different from some other knowledge, say scientific knowledge, in that it already involves a conceptual framework based on the concept of a person and the possibilities and expectations that stem therefrom. I need to know, however, something about the clues presented by persons. The most important of these is speech, but also included are things like the symbols and hints of movement and gesture. Some of these are widespread conventions in a given society, like nodding or shaking the head; others are conventions of a more limited circle, or even clues that I have come to recognize as the idiosyncracies of one person. We pick a lot of this up in a very *ad hoc* kind of way. We can 'read' some people we know well much better than we can strangers, but it seems quite unnecessary to use a word like empathy to describe this. It is important to realize that this kind of knowledge is never *just* of another person, it is always of another person or persons in certain observable or appraisable circumstances.

It must also be emphasized that what one is trying to do here is to come to know *how the other person conceives of the situation*, not how *I* would conceive of it were I in those circumstances. Certainly imagination is used, but it is not simply imagining my feelings and knowledge in the situation. It is rather an attempt to imagine what it is to be the other person in the situation. Indeed, the limitation of the original meaning of 'empathy' lay in that it named the projection of the observer into what is observed in order to give it meaning. Whilst this might make some sense when we look at pictures, it can be dangerously fallacious when we look at people.

If the argument so far is correct then we are now in a position to say that we do not need to posit sympathy or empathy as necessary to an account of knowing or understanding others, or to a description of basic concern for others. Instead, we can sum up the necessities for such a framework of knowledge and concern thus:

1 Possession of the concept of a person as a rational living body.

2 Possession of the family of concepts describing the attributes of a rational living body: consciousness, reason, intentionality, freedom of choice, responsibility, capacity for suffering and pleasure both physical and mental.

3 Possession of the concept of respect for persons, not merely in that one can use the phrase intelligently, but more importantly in *actually treating persons as persons*, that is, treating people as possessors of the attributes listed in 2.

4 Possession of a stock of knowledge and experience of the range of possibilities of human action, a range of imaginable possibilities in inter-personal life. The wider this knowledge and experience the more sensitive and aware one's moral and inter-personal life can be; but some minimal awareness of possibilities is necessary for any inter-personal or moral judgement at all.

5 Possession of the ability to appraise a situation or circumstance from the point of view of another involved person, and the ability to interpret the clues presented by others in voice, gesture and expression, or in action, so as to understand *their* conception of things. Again, this is a matter of degree, the better the skill the better the moral sensitivity; but some minimal skill at recognizing the point of view of the other is necessary to any moral judgement and action.

SECTION 6
Some implications of this account for Education

The main advantages to education lie in the fact that this account allows an approach to moral and inter-personal education which is primarily cognitive and has no reliance on conditioning of attitudes or the arousal of emotions by extrinsic motivation. In other words, in teaching children *about* persons we can also treat the children *as* persons.

This analysis also indicates a large and important area of the curriculum which would cluster about the idea of persons, their attributes and relationships. Such a rationale probably lies at the heart of that group of studies called the humanities. An important distinction to bear in mind, and to develop in the minds of pupils, is that between studying human beings as objects of science, for example, biology, psychology and sociology, where causal laws are sought and hypothesized; and studying human beings as persons, where reason, intentions and free will are taken as given in the very concepts (persons) that we are dealing with. To explain the latter in terms of the former would be the crudest kind of category mistake. Indeed, the trouble with some social studies courses in schools is the confusion of a kind of social *science* approach, needing one kind of conceptualization, with a *person* based approach, which needs another kind of conceptualization of the kind described above.

The curriculum area picked out as the group of studies built around the concept of a person would include moral education but would not be identical or co-extensive with it. Moral education, whilst requiring all the contributions that could be made to knowledge and understanding of persons and inter-personal relationships or situations, would need emphasis upon the treatment of persons *as* persons; emphasis, that is, upon respect for persons.

It might be objected that this only provides a minimal sense of moral education. Saints and heroes will never be produced like this, one might argue. It is very difficult, however, to see what justification can be given for deliberately setting out to produce saints and heroes, welcome though a few of them might be. It is even more difficult to know how to go about producing such characters. Telling children about saints and heroes as illustrative of normal morality could well do more harm than good by setting the aims of the moral life too high. What we want is the basis of accepted moral responsibility, based on a largely logical and cognitive framework of thought and action involving people, coherently related to other studies about persons, and providing ordinary people with guiding criteria in their everyday lives. The moral is to be seen as ordinary, not special; for all, not merely some; and as reasonably implied in the way we normally conceive of other persons and ourselves.

Summary

It is argued in this essay that problems central to moral education and social education involve the ideas of knowing others and having concern for others. These two ideas have often been discussed in terms of sympathy and empathy but such terms appear to present confusions and ambiguities which add to the problems rather than aid clarification or solution.

An alternative approach suggests working outwards from the concept of a person towards the implications of having such a conception. Education in this area would then avoid indoctrinating and conditioning-of-attitudes approaches, by operating at a level of cognition and reason which would involve helping pupils to develop certain concepts and to come to see the implications for behaviour appropriate to such conceptualization.

Further Reading

SECTION 1

Discussion of knowledge of others and concern for others as elements is moral education is to be found, for example, in Bull (1969) and in Wilson, Williams and Sugarman (1967). These ideas also figure largely in the work of the Schools Council Moral Education Curriculum Project as described by McPhail, Ungoed-Thomas and Chapman (1972).

SECTION 2

An extended discussion of the notion of empathy is to be found in Edith Stein's book (1964). Stein writes from a phenomenological point of view and it is this tradition that has most to say about the problems involved. Some discussion of the counselling and psychological approach to empathy appears in the work of Halmos (1965).

SECTION 3

In connection with the idea of sympathy a contrast may be made between the phenomenology of Max Scheler (1954) and a more recent discussion by Philip Mercer (1972). Downie and Telfer (1969) also attach considerable importance to a special view of sympathy in their account of respect for persons.

SECTION 5

Much of this section derives from emphasizing the centrality of the concept of a person. Langford (1970) discusses this in an elementary way. More detailed argument and debate can be found in Puccetti (1968), in Downie and Telfer and in the collection of papers edited by R. Ruddock (1972). An extended account of respect for persons is given in R. S. Peters (1966). Much recent debate on the concept of a person has been influenced by Strawson (1959).

7

Education and International Understanding

DAVID BRIDGES

SECTION I
Introduction

'In most parts of the world today, thinking men and women share the conviction that if the human species is to survive it will need to achieve a world perspective, that is to say, an understanding and a tolerance, if not a sympathy, for the innumerable traditions and patterns of behaviour found throughout the world. Teachers at every level of education increasingly ought to view their profession in an international context; to strive to foster in their pupils an awareness of supranational loyalties as the necessary condition for the legitimate fulfilment of national ones. Such education for international understanding must concern itself, not only with man's political and economic activities but also with the basic beliefs he holds about his own nature'. (Boyle and Lauwerys, in Lyall, 1967, p. ix.)

Major disasters or threats of disaster over the last seventy years have shocked the hitherto characteristically ethnocentric peoples of planet earth into attempts at mutual understanding and cooperation. International orgies of war have been succeeded by periods of sober reflection during which nations have sworn to secure fuller, happier, more sympathetic and more peaceful understanding between the peoples of the world. Perhaps despairing of the ignorance, prejudice and antipathies of their own generation, they have looked to the new generation, children, to build the better world of the future, and to their education to equip them for this not inconsiderable task. Hence—or at least this is *part* of the story—'education for international understanding'.

That education should contribute in some way to international understanding is a cause to which all signatories to the United Nations Charter have been pledged for many years. The Preamble to the Constitution of UNESCO declares:

'The States party to this Constitution, believing in full and equal opportunities for education for all, in the unrestricted pursuit of objective
truth, and in the free exchange of ideas and knowledge, are agreed and
determined to develop and to increase the means of communication
between their peoples and to employ these means for the purpose of
mutual understanding and a truer and more perfect knowledge of each
other's lives'.

On the whole it has been left to a handful of patient and persistent
idealists to translate the easily made promises of the governors into the
actual experience of the governed.

The last few years, however, have seen many developments which
indicate that education for international understanding in some sense will
be an increasing part of the experience of children in many parts of the
world. The international political, military and economic anxieties,
engagements and frustrations of the United States have provoked in that
country the establishment of numerous political and/or educational foundations with aims connected with securing through new patterns of teaching
and curriculum the development of new 'international understanding'
and/or 'world order'. In Great Britain the Council for Education in World
Citizenship has had a steady influence on the work of secondary
schools in particular. The quarterly *World Studies Bulletin* reports a wide
range of interest in 'world studies' throughout the education system—an
interest obviously reflected in the widening international coverage in 'O'
level and C.S.E. history courses and in the increasingly popular courses in
multi-disciplinary comparative or regional (e.g. oriental, Scandinavian,
Latin American or European) studies offered by universities. In the Autumn
of 1972 the One World Trust, sponsored by a Leverhulme grant of £24,000,
established a World Studies Project with the explicit objective 'to devise,
test and evaluate courses encouraging a world perspective, not only in
schools in this country but overseas as well'. (Shirley Williams M.P.
reported in *World Studies Bulletin*, No. 25, December 1972.)

The extension of the European Economic Community to include
Britain, Eire and Denmark has already provoked the predictable demand
that education should contribute more substantially to the development of
a fuller and closer understanding between the partner nations of this
Community. Even as Britain makes this move, however, her leaders
promise that this is to be seen as a step towards not merely the consolidation
of an exclusive club for Europeans but a wider and even global society.

Perhaps then this is not an inappropriate moment to pause and ask just
what this international understanding is to which education is supposed
in some way to contribute. If only we could be a bit clearer about what

education for international understanding is (on a global or merely European scale) we might have more idea of how it could best be pursued or whether indeed it should be pursued at all. This essay is an attempt at such a clarification.

The first thing which has to be made clear is that international understanding represents not one but several interconnected but distinguishable ideas. For the purposes of this discussion it will be useful to distinguish four. Three of these pick out cognitive and conceptual attainments, which we are urged to acquire. These are:

(i) international understanding in the sense of knowledge and understanding which people of different nations should have about each other's societies;

(ii) international understanding in the sense of knowledge about things international—about international relations, systems of world order, international and supranational organizations and institutions; and

(iii) international understanding as a characterization of the kind of understanding we should have of, for example, our own lives, our moral responsibilities, historical explanation—an understanding, that is, with the mark of a world or global perspective.

It is the conceptual and cognitive attainments as I have referred to them which I shall be concerned to examine in this essay. There is however a fourth sense of international understanding. That is the social and political attainment of *an* understanding—an agreement, settlement, peace, concord —among nations. I have already suggested that the establishment of international understanding in this sense is one of the main reasons (though it is *not* the only reason) for the concern that international understanding in the cognitive senses already referred to should have a place among curriculum objectives. However, this issue, along with this sense of international understanding, will remain outside the scope of the present essay. Here I shall discuss only the sort of *cognitive* attainments which are picked out by the concept of international understanding.

SECTION 2
International Understanding in the sense of knowledge and understanding we should have of other societies

'In education for international understanding, we should try to promote a comprehension of the ways of life, the values, and the aspirations of all peoples of the world'. (Long and King, 1964, p. 24.) This sentiment echoes the ambition set out in the Preamble to the U.N.E.S.C.O. Constitution to which I have already referred: 'The States parties to this Constitution . . . are agreed and determined to develop and to increase the means of communication between their peoples and to employ these means for the purposes of mutual understanding and a truer and more perfect knowledge of each other's lives.' In an earlier contribution to this volume (see chapter 4, p. 64 ff. above) I tried to begin an account of what understanding another society might involve as a matter of priority. I suggested:

(a) *a priori* knowledge of the nature of societies in general and hence of the kind of enquiry appropriate to their explication;

(b) (on a certain view of the nature of society) knowledge of the rules and conventions under which members of the society saw themselves as acting;

(c) knowledge of the form taken in the particular society of the 'limiting concepts' or 'constants' of human experience.

Further explanation of these points may be found in my preceding essay. I shall not elaborate on them further in this context—but simply note that a concern that we should come to understand other societies is a central feature of the literature about international understanding. Accounts of what might be constitutive of such understanding, however, are somewhat rarer.

There is one question which I should raise here. Presumably we are not really expected to teach for an understanding of 'the ways of life, the values and the aspirations of all peoples in the world', as Long and King suggest? This is simply not a realistic ambition. But if we are not to teach about them all, then which of the many nations and societies of the world should we seek, as a matter of priority, to understand—those that we find most interesting? Those most radically different from our own? Those having most dealings with our own? Those affecting and influencing most others? On what basis are we to choose? It is clear neither in the more general literature on education and international understanding, nor in the detailed syllabuses which are sometimes put forward what principle of selection does or should apply.

SECTION 3
International Understanding in the sense of knowledge and understanding of international organizations and international relations

In some of the literature in this field teachers are encouraged to provide their pupils with an understanding not only of other societies or other nations, but also of international and supranational bodies. The

U.N.E.S.C.O. Associated Schools Project, for example, sets 'teaching about the United Nations' as the first of three main themes proposed to all schools taking part in the scheme (U.N.E.S.C.O., 1959 forward). The case for teaching the detailed constitution and workings of the United Nations and the World Bank at school level is rarely pressed very hard, except perhaps by the U.N. itself. It has however been considered important that people should realize that 'the world community has its skeletal structure' in the form of the rapidly growing number of international organizations (Goodings and Lauwerys, 1964, p. 5). One of the central objectives listed in the Foreign Policy Association Report is 'an understanding of the world system, which would include . . . an understanding of the international or global social system as *one* level of human social organizations'. This is taken to involve 'studies of the inter-nation system, cross national organizations and businesses, war, trade, communication and major international social phenomena'. (King, 1971, p. 26.)

The new curriculum ingredient which is commonly recommended, especially in some of the American literature in this field, is the teaching of some fairly sophisticated form of study of international relations. What we are urged to do however is something rather different from the element of 'foreign affairs' in the traditional history syllabus. Typically, its aspiration is to be 'scientific' or at least 'social scientific' in character. It is concerned with projection into the future, and not just reflection on the past. And it is overtly directed towards the solution of contemporary world conflict. This is what Saul Mendlovitz has called 'the emerging discipline of world order'. Betty Reardon explains this 'discipline' as follows: 'the control of international violence is the central problem of all world order studies and accounts for the problem-solving orientation of the discipline. Emphasis is placed on analysis and evaluations of actual and potential institutions to deal with the problem through the examination of alternative systems and proposals or 'models' . . . The most unique attributes of the discipline are its global and futuristic aspects . . .' (Reardon, 1967, p. 458.)

It would be quite improper to dismiss out of hand the case for 'an emerging discipline of world order' which has been represented so briefly and so partially. However, there are some general puzzles about what this discipline is trying to do which perhaps are worth mentioning briefly, for some of them will beleaguer *any* attempt at understanding 'international relations' or 'the international or global social system'.

First, it is not at all clear between whom or what international relations are imagined to take place. In what sense are they really conducted between 'nations'? Surely we are talking about negotiations between persons—diplomats, generals and ministers most commonly—who happen to have the authority which binds other members of their communities to accept whatever bargains they strike. These other people, the non-negotiators, may very possibly remain in total ignorance of the arrangements made on their behalf. Similarly, it is presumably the case that 'the international or global system' is in fact a set of persons who have various different kinds of relations between themselves—commercial, legal, cultural, academic and so on. If not, what sort of account *are* we to give of the 'global' system?

This is not just a trivial question of semantics. If, to take the first case, what we are trying to understand is how persons vested with certain authority by fellow members of their respective communities arrive at agreement, or why they see fit to disagree even to the point of bloody conflict, then I am not sure that the 'emerging discipline or world order' has been appropriately conceived. Let me summarize my doubts in this way: if it is *the activities of persons*, albeit persons vested with particular authority, which we are concerned to understand in this field of inter-national relations, then: (*a*) are concepts like 'institutions', 'systems', 'models', really the ones most likely to contribute to an understanding of their activities? (*b*) In what sense and how far into the heart of the matter, can we pursue an investigation into that activity which is 'scientific' in character? (*c*) Can we hope to predict with any degree of reliability their future activity?

These questions raise fundamental issues about the social sciences in general. It is important that this should be done, for some views of the study of inter-societal or international relations, and also some views of what is involved in understanding a society, are made unsatisfactory by a mis-categorization of 'persons' which is rooted in the basic assumptions of the social sciences themselves. The point is not that there is no place for the scientific investigation of the species homo sapiens and many aspects of his metabolism and behaviour; but that what is *central* to an understanding of the 'activity of persons' cannot be encompassed by this kind of investigation.

Perhaps I can highlight at least one of the problems embedded in the kind of study of international relations to which some social scientists aspire by indicating some of the implications of my third sceptical question: can we hope to predict with any reliability the future activity of persons?

Anyone can make predictions about what will happen in the future; the difficulty is in making reasonably *correct* predictions as to what will happen. When we are trying to predict the future activity of persons, this becomes particularly difficult, because what a person does is usually based on some kind of appraisal of the situation in which he finds himself; in other words, the knowledge he has affects the course of action he will take (see Popper, 1960, for many points in this argument). If he knows that the ice will break if he walks on it, he will normally avoid walking on it. Without this knowledge he might very well have walked across it and fallen into the pond. What makes reliable prediction of people's actions almost infinitely complex if not logically imponderable is the fact that the prediction itself brings about a change in the knowledge available, a change in the situation with reference to which a prediction was made, and consequently some likelihood of change in the course of action which someone is most likely to take. The man to whom it is foretold that he will walk across the partially frozen pond and fall in, will, if he has any wit about him, avoid the pond and thus refute the prediction. If it is persuasively predicted that share prices will rise next month then investors will buy this month and the inflation will begin prematurely. (Just to make matters more complicated, this statement of course is also a prediction which could further alter the situation!) Confident 'prediction' is a method used both to make things happen which even the predictor knows might well not have happened but for the prediction—'fashionable men will be wearing ex-army boots next spring'; and to avoid things which might well have happened but for the prediction—'the inevitable outcome of the present build-up of arms will be a nuclear holocaust'. Even what are intended as self-refuting or self-fulfilling predictions are not reliable guides to what will or will not happen. For again, once it is known that this is what they are, the situation changes. In any case the cussed element in human nature drives some people to confound prophecy and some people to pre-empt it.

There is a marked distinction here between what happens when one attempts predictions about persons and what happens when one attempts predictions about things. A person is affected by the announcement that a boulder will fall down and crush him. The information is likely to produce avoiding action on his part. The prediction radically affects the situation and what happens in it. If the same was predicted of a wooden hut, a tin can or a flowering plant, however, these objects and the predicted event would be quite unaffected, unless, of course, some person intervened who had an interest in saving one or other of them from destruction.

I cannot give a systematic critique of the social sciences as an aside to a subsection of an essay on another topic. In any case, I do not wish to deny the possibility of scientific scrutiny of man's behaviour. Ayer, in *Man as a subject for Science* (1967) and Gibson, in *The Logic of Social Enquiry* (1960), have met many of the more sweeping and facile objections to such an activity. Nevertheless, it is important to question the capacity of scientific enquiry *alone* to encompass all that is to be understood, or even what is central to an understanding, of the activities of persons. The discussion of the possibility of predicting human activities merely illustrates one of the special difficulties presented when we have a reflective being as the subject for study.

This, however, is only one example out of many complex problems raised by the pursuit of an understanding of social phenomena such as other societies, the 'global' society or inter-societal or international relations. The general point that I have tried to illustrate is that it is not at all clear, when it comes down to any degree of specificity what those pursuits or their attainments would involve. The assumption that a full, real or correct understanding of human social phenomena is obtainable through 'scientific' enquiry is—at least—controversial.

SECTION 4
International Understanding as a characterization of the way in which we should understand things, as a world perspective

The Education Advisory Committee to the Parliamentary Group for World Government describes its aim as 'to encourage a dual perspective in education—world as well as national—so that opportunity is given in the curriculum for balancing national loyalty with a measure of conscious loyalty to the human race as a whole in all its diversity'. (Parliamentary Group for World Government, 1968, p. 5.)

Hilda Taba begins to spell out more fully what this new perspective should be like. Men must learn, she writes, 'to escape their own narrow, personal and ethnocentric perspectives'. She warns against 'the dangers of ethnocentricity embedded in the natural socialization of any culture'; and remarks that 'although living in a world of vastly expanded horizons requires a vastly extended sensitivity and capacity to understand, there is little in the usual curriculum of our public schools that is addressed directly to developing a cosmopolitan sensitivity, to seeing the 'culturally other' in its own right . . . The curriculum should develop the knowledge and perspective which is commensurate with the kind of world in which we live'. (Taba, 1962, pp. 46, 73 and 273.)

Still on the same theme, Althea Lyall (in *History Syllabuses and a World Perspective*) describes how any episode in history can be seen in this world perspective: 'one method, used instinctively by most gifted teachers, is to show any event of national, local or continental import as an extension of human experience and therefore of universal significance. Another approach is to see sectional history from a global point of view; in this way way some causes which loom large in chauvinist mythology disappear into triviality whilst others take on a new more widely salient aspect'. (Lyall, 1967, p. xiii.)

The idea running through these three passages is that it is important for us to have a 'world perspective'. The pieces quoted give some idea of what a world perspective would be, but do not add up to an entirely coherent or specific account. Let me attempt to move one step nearer to such an account by spelling out in a little more detail what this 'world perspective' might entail.

There is first of all one way in which the notion of a world perspective is used which can be dealt with fairly briefly. This is where what is recommended is simply knowledge about all the major parts of the world. 'A world perspective on religion' can mean a quantity of information about each of the world's major religions. 'History with a world perspective' may simply involve doing a bit of history about each of the major world civilizations.

On the whole, however, what most of the literature on the subject seems to be getting at is something rather more ambitious and interesting than this. David King specifically rejects what he calls the 'strange-lands-and-friendly-people' approach and endorses the view of the Foreign Policy Association Study that 'what we need is *not* a greater proliferation of culture studies or units examining various events in the traditional relations of nation-states. To give students adequate preparation for today's world, the schools must help them to gain a global perspective'. (King, 1971, pp. 15 and 9.) I have in any case already discussed some of the problems connected with understanding other societies and in particular the issue of what knowledge about other societies should have priority; so I will leave this first interpretation of a world perspective with simply a mention and proceed to some of the other things which the slogan might involve.

A second interpretation of what it would be to have a world perspective might be 'being able to view life and the world under a national or cultural framework of values other than man's own'. This would be an extension of the idea of 'seeing the world as others see it'.

Hilda Taba explains the source of the deficiency which can be put right only through deliberate teaching of this world perspective: 'Socialization into one culture inevitably creates barriers to understanding the values of another culture. Because individuals are conditioned to the behaviour, values and norms of a given society, their capacity to understand and to appreciate that which is different from their own culture is limited. In addition to the difficulty of seeing the 'other', there is the culturally conditioned incapacity to see members of the other cultures in terms of that culture's values and standards. A person of one culture responds to a foreign culture in terms of the values and norms of his own culture—that is to say, ethnocentrically'. (Taba, 1962, pp. 51–52.) In place of this ethnocentricity, Taba wants all individuals to develop 'a sensitivity which permits them to explore sympathetically and realistically the frame of mind, feelings and values out of which persons with a different orientation think and act'. (Ibid, p. 56.)

Now there may be some puzzles as to the nature of this 'sensitivity' which

Taba wants us to acquire, but let us ignore those, and assume that there is an attainment which we can aspire to which is something like seeing the world in the perspective of the values, the conventions, the *weltanschaung* of another culture. And let us say also that we can gain this kind of understanding, this way of seeing things, for a whole number of different cultures. Does this add up to a world perspective?

It seems to me that it does not. At least, it might be what *some* people understand by a world perspective. But others would say that the ambition that people should master more than one ethnocentric way of looking at the world, admirable though it is, falls short of what can properly be called a world perspective. What is conceived (and this is my third interpretation of the concept) is a perspective which transcends even a plurality of other ethnocentric views, a perspective which is truly *global*. Surely it is nothing short of this which James Henderson has in mind in those exciting passages from *Education for World Understanding*:

> 'Man has to rediscover and live from that third element in all human personality which is the seat of the species' shared value . . . "the mid-point of the Self" (Jung) or as Lewis Mumford once described it, "the Self that we share with our fellows". (Henderson, 1968, p. 11.)

> 'The supreme purpose of education for world understanding is to enable man to identify and reverence that which today concerns them all ultimately as human beings'. (Ibid., p. 27.)

> 'Education for world understanding consists in building a church in which men of all faiths can worship and in nourishing a conscience recognizable as being that of the human race'. (Ibid., p. 148.)

In at least some of the 'world understanding' literature, then, it is not merely a plurality of ethnocentric perspectives which we are urged to pursue, but a unified overriding global perspective.

This is an interesting but puzzling idea. It is not altogether clear whether this world view is already supposed to be available to us in some way, already clearly articulated in a set of norms, conventions, rules, values, concepts, etc., equivalent in its relation to the world society to the more familiar sets of norms, etc. which characterize our more limited national and other societies (see above p. 67); or whether this world view is in fact something we are urged to evolve and create in some way, possibly as the foundation-stone of a world society properly so called. Either way, the case is an obscure one. If such a world view is already available to us what are its features and where is it to be found? If such a view is not yet evolved, then how are its features to be defined?

Henderson is one of the few writers who even begin to tackle these, admittedly profoundly difficult, questions. The passages already quoted indicate something of the tenor of his argument. The world perspective is to be sought, it seems, in 'our psychological and spiritual origins' (Henderson, 1968, p. 63); in 'collective memories of mankind' (p. 125); in 'the consciousness of the universal in man' (p. 13); in what Bozeman calls 'those moments in recorded time in which men of different continents and cultures succeed in transcending their local environments'. (Quoted in Henderson, 1968, p. 12.)

If these phrases are seminal and intriguing, they are also systematically mysterious. They have a certain poetic grandeur of style but an elusive sense or meaning. They seem better designed to inspire than to inform, but though we certainly need inspiration, it will soon flag without intelligible purpose and direction.

Perhaps some of the features of the next two interpretations will bring us close to at least a partial conception of that purpose.

In a fourth interpretation, we could say that somebody had a world perspective if he were able, where relevant, to describe the course of events, the problems, aspirations and concerns of one society in terms of causes, consequences and general movements which lay outside that society. It would be argued that the more extensive the dealings and interaction between different nations, the more crucial this perspective becomes to any true understanding of the problem under investigation. Given the present structure of international trade and finance, for example, fluctuations in the British economy are unintelligible within a framework of explanation which does not take into consideration events in Wall Street, Zurich, or the E.E.C. The causes and consequences of the events inside Berlin in 1948, Hungary in 1956 or Cuba in 1962 need to be looked for far beyond the frontiers of these communities. The concerns of Britain, Burma or Brazil with the control of disease and the most profitable exploitation of the world's resources are not realizable through the isolated and individual enterprise of any of those individual states alone; nor is a proper understanding of the problems involved to be gained through a scrutiny of conditions in any one of these societies.

It has been argued that it is not merely in the study of contemporary society that a world perspective is required. Court, for example, suggests that, 'The history of the economic development of one nation almost always requires the economic history of other peoples to make it fully intelligible ... a student of English economic history is, almost by definition, a student of the economic history of Europe and more than Europe over periods of time which deepen with his purposes'. (Finberg, 1962, pp. 43–4.)

Without the sort of wider perspective I have described, one could have *an* understanding of certain events, but, on the view I am setting out, it would be a partial, incomplete or even mistaken understanding.

This view seems to be thoroughly acceptable provided that it is not pushed too far. Some events clearly require an explanation and have consequences which go far beyond national frontiers. But this is obviously not the case with all events, as a glance at some of our local newspapers will surely demonstrate. Nor has it always been so much the case as perhaps it is today.

This is not to say that apparently the most parochial of events might not be endowed with a kind of universal significance, but I am immediately concerned to examine a rather different claim.

The idea of perspective is closely related to that of proportion both in art and in the assessment of our experiences. Thus when someone seems unduly upset by a relatively trivial disappointment we urge them 'to get things into proper proportion', or synonymously, to 'put things into a true perspective', and we mean that we want them to see the things which are important and the things which are trivial in their proper relationship.

A world perspective is, in one sense, an extension of this idea. It contains both the notion of a scale of values, priorities or importance—a perspective; and a criterion on which those values, priorities or judgements might be based—something like, 'that which concerns most nearly the world as a whole'. To approach history with a world perspective in this sense would be to select for study those movements and events which affected the largest part of the world's population, with the result that, as Althea Lyall anticipates, 'some causes which loom large in chauvinist mythology disappear into triviality whilst others take on a new more widely salient aspect'. (Lyall, 1967, p. xiii.) To apply a world perspective of this kind to decisions about the development of the world's natural resources would be to judge not 'what contributes most to the prosperity of my nation' but rather 'what contributes most to the prosperity of all nations'. In a world perspective that which would be most important or most highly valued would be that which most closely touched the interest not of myself, nor even of my country, but of the whole world. This is the fifth idea which appears to be contained in the notion of a world perspective.

It is important to make a distinction here. We might be urged to *know how to apply* the sort of perspective I have described, that is simply to know what it would be to judge or discriminate according to these criteria. This would be an exhortation to particular knowledge or understanding. But also we might be urged to *apply* this sort of criterion in our own judgements. This would be an exhortation to a particular set of values and would clearly involve a much more extended commitment.

Summary

I have tried to suggest something of the range of attainments which seem to be contained in the notion of education for international understanding.

SECTION 1

I outlined some of the background to the current concern with education for international understanding and suggested that the time was ripe for closer analysis of the concept.

SECTION 2

An account was offered of the concept of international understanding in terms of the knowledge and understanding we should have of other societies. This, in turn, was interpreted in terms of:

(a) *a priori* knowledge of the nature of societies in general and hence of the kinds of enquiry appropriate to their explication;

(b) (on a particular view of the nature of society) knowledge of the rules and conventions under which members of the society saw themselves as acting;

(c) knowledge of the form taken in the particular society of the 'limiting concepts' or 'constants' of human experience.

SECTION 3

I interpreted international understanding in terms of knowledge and understanding of international organizations and international relations. This section raised some questions about attempts to make the study of these relations in any proper sense of the word 'scientific'.

SECTION 4

I tried to explore different conceptions of what it would be to have 'a world perspective' which, it was suggested, was another way in which the goal of education for international understanding might be set out. It was suggested that having a world perspective might entail any or all of the following:

(i) knowing about all the (major?) parts of the world, or, for example in 'history with a world perspective', knowing about the history of all the major parts of the world;

(ii) knowing how to interpret the world in the perspective of the values and conventions of a number of different cultures;

(iii) knowing how to interpret the world under some kind of unified global perspective, which in relation to the incipient world society would be equivalent to the more familiar sets of norms, etc. which underlie our present national societies;

(iv) knowing how, where relevant, to describe a course of events or a problem, identified in one society in terms of causes, consequences or general movements which lie outside that society;

(v) knowing how to judge what is most important, most significant or most highly to be valued in terms of what most closely touches the interests, not necessarily of myself, nor even of my country, but of the whole world.

Of course, not all references to a world perspective are intended to be references to all the components that I have pointed out. One problem is that few of the sources clearly distinguish between these rather different ideas.

Analysis of what *might* be involved in international understanding reveals a very wide range of cognitive attainments (not to mention the political ones). Those who urge that education should contribute to international understanding could helpfully specify rather more closely just what it is they are calling upon us to secure. Close definition of international understanding could enable us to see more clearly why or whether this should be an urgent concern for educators. If we decided that international understanding should indeed be our urgent concern, the same closer definition of our objectives could then help us to see more easily how our adopted cause could most effectively be won.

Governments which declare that world order, cooperation and peace must be based on developing a reciprocal international understanding, might better persuade us of their attachment to that world order if they were more energetic in their promotion of efforts to define the elements of that understanding and make them more readily accessible to new generations of citizens.

If this understanding has one quarter of the significance these governments declare it to have, it should be pursued with the very greatest urgency. The claim that the survival of the species is at stake may not be an exaggeration.

Further Reading

It is not easy to offer anything other than rather general references for further reading in relation to this chapter.

The fullest and most interesting advocacy of education for international understanding is to be found in J. L. Henderson's work (1968); in a wide range of contributions to the *1964 Yearbook of Education* edited by Bereday and Lauwerys (1964); and, more recently, by David C. King (1971). This last book provides in the most accessible form for British readers the main points of the report of the Foreign Policy Association (U.S.A.), *An Examination of Objectives, Needs and Priorities in International Education in U.S. Secondary and Elementary Schools*. Abstracts from some of the relevant official documents are collected in U.N.E.S.C.O. (1964). Hilda Taba (1962) has some interesting references to the dangers of 'ethnocentricity' and the importance of the development of a 'cosmopolitan sensitivity'.

Bibliography

ALLPORT, G. W. (1938) *Personality*. London: Constable.

ARISTOTLE (1962) *The Politics*. Harmondsworth: Penguin Classics.

ARGYLE, M. (1967) *The Psychology of Inter-personal Behaviour*. Harmondsworth: Penguin Books.

ATKIN, M. (1970) 'Behavioural objectives in curriculum design: a cautionary note.' In MARTIN, J. R. *Readings in the Philosophy of Education: a Study of Curriculum*. Boston: Allyn and Bacon.

AYER, A. J. (1967) 'Man as a subject for science.' In LASLETT, P. and RUNCIMAN, W. G. (eds.) *Philosophy, Politics and Society*, 3rd Series. Oxford: Basil Blackwell.

BAILEY, C. (1971) 'Rationality, democracy and the neutral teacher.' *Cambridge Journal of Education*, No. 2, Easter 1971.

BAILEY, C. (1973) 'Teaching by discussion and the neutral teacher.' *Proceedings of the Philosophy of Education Society of Great Britain*, Vol. VII, No. 1, January 1973. Oxford: Basil Blackwell.

BEARDSMORE, R. (1969) *Moral Reasoning*. London: Routledge and Kegan Paul.

BEREDAY, G. Z. F., and LAUWERYS, J. A. (1964) *The Yearbook of Education: Education and International Life*. London: Evans Bros.

BERNSTEIN, B. B. (1971) 'On the classification and framing of educational knowledge.' In YOUNG, M. (ed.) *Knowledge and Control*. New York: Crowell, Collier and Macmillan.

BOZEMAN, A. S. (1960) *Politics and Culture in International History*. Princeton: D. Van Nostrand.

BRADLEY, F. H. (1867) Essay 5 in *Ethical Studies*. Oxford: Oxford University Press.

BRODBECK, M. (ed.) (1968) *Readings in the Philosophy of the Social Sciences*. New York: Crowell, Collier and Macmillan.

BRUNER, J. S. (1960) *The Process of Education*. Cambridge, Mass.: Harvard University Press.

BRUNER, J. S. (1966) *Towards a Theory of Instruction*. Cambridge, Mass.: Harvard University Press.

BULL, N. J. (1969) *Moral Education*. London: Routledge and Kegan Paul.

CANNON, C. (1964) 'Social studies in secondary schools.' *Educational Review*, XVII (1), 1964.

CLARKE, Sir F. (1943) *Education and Social Change*. London: University of London Press.

CREBER, J. W. P. (1965) *Sense and Sensitivity*. London: University of London Press.

CREMIN, L. A. (1961) *The Transformation of the School*. New York: Knopf.

CROWTHER REPORT (1959) *15 to 18: Report of the Central Advisory Council for Education (England)*. Vol. 1. London: H.M.S.O.

DEARDEN, R. F. (1968) *The Philosophy of Primary Education*. London: Routledge and Kegan Paul.

DEWEY, J. (1916) *Democracy and Education*. New York: Macmillan.

DEWEY, J. (1938) *Logic: The Theory of Enquiry*. New York: Holt, Rinehart and Winston.

DOWNIE, R. S., and TELFER, E. (1969) *Respect for Persons*. London: George Allen and Unwin.

DURKHEIM, E. (1956) *Education and Sociology*. Blencoe, Illinois: Free Press.

EDUCATION DEVELOPMENT CENTER (1969) *Curiosity, Competence, Community*. Cambridge, Mass.: Education Development Center.

ELLIOTT, J. (1969) 'The role of the humanities in vocational education.' *Studies in Education and Craft*, Autumn 1969.

ELLIOTT, J. (1971) 'The concept of the neutral teacher.' *Cambridge Journal of Education*, No. 2, Easter 1971.

ELLIOTT, J. (ed.) (1972) *People and Work*. London: Heinemann Educational.

ELLIOTT, J. (1973) 'Neutrality, rationality and the role of the teacher.' *Proceedings of the Philosophy of Education Society of Great Britain*, Vol. VII, No. 1, January 1973. Oxford: Basil Blackwell.

ESTVAN, F. J. (1968) *Social Studies in a Changing World*. New York: Harcourt Brace.

FILMER, P. *et al.* (1972) *New Directions in Sociological Theory*. London: Collier-Macmillan.

FINBERG, H. P. R. (ed.) (1962) *Approaches in History*. London: Routledge and Kegan Paul.

FOREIGN POLICY ASSOCIATION (U.S.A.) (1971) *An Examination of Objectives, Needs and Priorities in International Education in U.S. Secondary and Elementary Schools*. New York: Foreign Policy Association.

GARDINER, P. (1952) *The Nature of Historical Explanation*. Oxford: Oxford University Press.

GIBSON, Q. (1960) *The Logic of Social Enquiry*. London: Routledge and Kegan Paul.

GINSBERG, M. (1968) 'On the diversity of morals.' In his *Essays in Sociology and Social Philosophy*. Harmondsworth: Penguin Books.

GOFFMAN, T. (1961) *Asylums*. Harmondsworth: Penguin Books.

GOODINGS, R. F., and LAUWERYS, J. A. (1964) 'Education and international life.' In BEREDAY, G. Z. F., and LAUWERYS, J. A. (eds.) *The Yearbook of Education: Education and International Life*. London: Evans Bros.

GORBUTT, D., BOWDEN, T., and PRING, R. (1972) 'Education as the control of knowledge.' In *Education for Teaching*, Autumn 1972, Journal of the Association of Teachers in Colleges and Departments of Education.

HALMOS, P. (1965) *The Faith of Counsellors*. London: Constable.

HAMINGSON, D. (ed.) (1973) *Towards Judgement: the Publications of the Evaluation Unit of the Humanities Project*. Centre for Applied Research in Education, University of East Anglia.

HARGREAVES, D. (1973) *Inter-personal Relations and Education*. London: Routledge and Kegan Paul.

HARGREAVES, D. (1967) *Social Relations in a Secondary School*. London: Routledge and Kegan Paul.

HANVEY, R. (1971) 'The Social Studies, the Educational Culture and the State.' In EISNER, E. W. (ed.) *Confronting Curriculum Reform*. Boston, Mass.: Little, Brown.

HENDERSON, J. L. (1968) *Education for World Understanding*. Oxford: Pergamon.

HIRST, P. H. (1965) 'Liberal education and the nature of knowledge.' In ARCHAMBAULT, R. D. (ed.) *Philosophical Analysis and Education*. London: Routledge and Kegan Paul.

HOLBROOK, D. (1967) *English for Maturity*. Cambridge: Cambridge University Press.

HOLLIS, M. (1968) 'Reason and ritual.' In *Philosophy*, Vol. XLII.

HUME, D. (ed. MOSSNER, E. C.) (1969) *A Treatise of Human Nature*. Harmondsworth: Penguin Books.

JACKSON, P. W. (1968) *Life in Classrooms*. New York: Holt, Rinehart and Winston.

KILPATRICK, W. H. (ed.) (1933) *The Education Frontier*. New York: Century.

KING, D. C. (1971) *International Education for Spaceship Earth*. New York: Foreign Policy Association.

KLEIN, J. (1963) *Working with Groups*. London: Hutchinson.

LANGFORD, G. (1970) *Philosophy and Education*. London: Macmillan.

LONG, H. M., and KING, R. N. (1964) *Improving the Teaching of World Affairs—the Glens Falls Story*. Washington: National Council for Social Studies (U.S.A.).

LYALL, A. (ed.) (1967) *History Syllabuses and a World Perspective*, 2nd Edition. London: Longmans and Parliamentary Group for World Government.

MACDONALD, B. (1967) *Evaluation of the Humanities Curriculum Project: a Wholistic Approach*, (Interim Report). Unpublished.

MacIntyre, A. (1967) *A Short History of Ethics*. London: Routledge and Kegan Paul.

McMullen, T. (1970) 'The clarification of aims and objectives as an aid to making decisions. In Taylor, G. *The Teacher as Manager*. London: National Council for Educational Technology.

McPhail, P., Ungoed-Thomas, J. R., and Chapman, H. (1972) *Moral Education in Secondary Schools*. London: Longmans.

Mercer, P. (1972) *Sympathy and Ethics*. Oxford: Oxford University Press.

Morrisett, I. (1967) *Concepts and Structure in the New Social Curricula*. New York: Holt, Rinehart and Winston.

Morrison, A., and McIntyre, D. (eds.) (1972) *Social Psychology of Teaching*. Harmondsworth: Penguin Books.

Nagel, E. (1961) *The Structure of Science*. London: Routledge and Kegan Paul.

National Society for the Study of Education (1926) *Twenty-sixth Year Book*, Vols. I and II: Report of the Joint Committee. Vol. I, 'Curriculum Past and Present.' Vol. II, 'The foundations of curriculum making.' Chicago: University of Chicago Press.

Newson Report (1963) *Half our Future*. Report of the Central Advisory Council for Education (England). London: H.M.S.O.

Oakeshott, M. (1962) 'The voice of poetry in the conversation of mankind.' In his *Rationalism in Politics*. London: Methuen.

Oakeshott, M. (1972) 'Education: the engagement and its frustrations.' In *Proceedings of the Philosophy of Education Society*, Vol. VIII (1).

Parker, J. C. and Rubin, L. J. (1966) *Process as Content: Curriculum Design and the Application of Knowledge*. Chicago: University of Chicago Press.

Parliamentary Group for World Government (1968) *World Wise*. London: Parliamentary Group for World Government.

Peters, R. S. (1963) *Authority, Responsibility and Education*. London: George Allen and Unwin.

Peters, R. S. (1966) *Ethics and Education*. London: George Allen and Unwin.

Peters, R. S. (1973) 'Aims of Education—a conceptual enquiry.' In Peters, R. S. (ed.) *The Philosophy of Education*. Oxford: Oxford University Press.

Philip, W., and Priest, R. (1965) *Social Science and Social Studies in Secondary Schools*. London: Longmans.

Phenix, P. (1958) *Realms of Meaning*. New York: Holt, Rinehart and Winston.

Phillips, D. Z., and Mounce, H. O. (1969) *Moral Practices*. London: Routledge and Kegan Paul.

Piaget, J. (1932) *The Moral Judgement of the Child*. London: Routledge and Kegan Paul.

POLE, D. (1958) *The Later Philosophy of Wittgenstein*. London: Athlone Press of the University of London.

POPHAM, W. J. (1969) 'Objectives and instruction,' *A.E.R.A. Monograph Series on Curriculum Evaluation*, No. 3. Chicago: Rand McNally.

POPPER, K. (1960) *The Poverty of Historicism*. 2nd Edition. London: Routledge and Kegan Paul.

POPPER, K. (1963) *Conjectures and Refutations: the Growth of Scientific Knowledge*. London: Routledge and Kegan Paul.

PUCCETTI, R. (1968) *Persons*. London: Macmillan.

REARDON, B. (1967) 'The World Law Fund: world approach to international education.' In *Teachers' College Record* Vol. 68, No. 6, March 1967.

ROGERS, V. (ed.) (1968) *Social Studies in Education*. London: Heinemann.

RUDD, A. (1970) 'Curriculum model building.' In BUTCHER, H. J., and PONT, H. B. *Educational Research in Britain II*. London: University of London Press.

RUDDUCK, J. (1972) 'Man: a course of study.' *Cambridge Journal of Education*, Easter Term 1972, pp. 118–26.

RUDDUCK, R. (ed.) (1972) *Six Approaches to the Person*. London: Routledge and Kegan Paul.

RYLE, G. (1963) *The Concept of Mind*. Harmondsworth: Penguin Books.

SCHEFFLER, I. (1960) *The Language of Education*. Springfield, Illinois: Thomas.

SCHELER, M. (1954) *The Nature of Sympathy*. London: Routledge and Kegan Paul.

SCHOOLS COUNCIL

> Working Paper No. 2 *Raising the School Leaving Age: a cooperative programme of research and development* (H.M.S.O., 1965)
>
> Working Paper No. 11 *Society and the Young School Leaver: a humanities programme in preparation for the raising of the school leaving age* (H.M.S.O., 1967)
>
> Working Paper No. 12 *The Educational Implications of Social and Economic Change* (H.M.S.O., 1967)
>
> Working Paper No. 17 *Community Service and the Curriculum* (H.M.S.O., 1968)
>
> Working Paper No. 22 *The Middle Years of Schooling* (H.M.S.O., 1969)
>
> Working Paper No. 27 *'Crossed with Adversity': the education of socially disadvantaged children in secondary schools* (H.M.S.O., 1970)
>
> Working Paper No. 39 *Social Studies 8–13* (H.M.S.O., 1972)
>
> Working Paper No. 40 *Careers Education in the 1970s* (Evans/Methuen, 1972)
>
> Welsh Committee *Another Year—to endure or enjoy?* (H.M.S.O., 1967)

SKILBECK, M. (1968) *Curriculum Development: The Nature of the Task.* Unpublished.

SMITH, A. (1964) 'The theory of moral sentiment.' In SELBY-BIGGE, L. A. (ed.) *British Moralists.* New York: Bobs-Merrill.

SMITH, B. O., STANLEY, W. O., and SHORES, J. H. (1957) *Fundamentals of Curriculum Development.* New York: Harcourt, Brace and World

SMITH, R. I. (ed.) (1968) *Men and Societies.* London: Heinemann.

SOCKETT, H. T. (1972) 'Curriculum aims and objectives: taking a means to an end.' In *Proceedings of the Philosophy of Education Society of Great Britain*, Vol. VI, No. 1.

SOCKETT, H. T. (1973) 'Behavioural objectives.' In *London Educational Review*, Vol. II, No. 3, Autumn 1973.

STEIN, E. (1964) *On the Problem of Empathy.* The Hague: Martinus Nijhoff.

STEINBERG, I. (1972) 'Behavioural definition of educational objectives.' In *National Society for the Study of Education Yearbook, Part 1, Philosophical Direction of Educational Research.* Chicago: University of Chicago Press.

STENHOUSE, L. S. (1970) 'Controversial value issues in the classroom.' In CARR, W. G. (ed.) *Values and the Curriculum: a Report of the Fourth International Curriculum Conference.* Washington: National Education Association.

STENHOUSE, L. S. et al. (1970) *The Humanities Project: an Introduction.* London: Heinemann Educational.

STENHOUSE, L. S. (1970–1) 'Some limitations of the use of objectives in curriculum research and planning.' In *Paedagogica Europea 6.*

STENHOUSE, L. S. (1971) 'The idea of neutrality.' In *The Times Educational Supplement*, 4th February 1971.

STRAWSON, P. (1959) *Individuals.* London: Methuen.

TABA, H. (1962) *Curriculum Development: Theory and Practice.* New York: Harcourt Brace.

TABA, H. (1967) *Teachers' Handbook for Elementary Social Studies.* Reading, Mass.: Addison-Wesley.

TAYLOR, P. H. (1970) *Curriculum Planning for Compensatory Education—a Suggested Procedure.* London: Schools Council.

TYLER, R. W. (1947) *Basic Principles of Curriculum and Instruction.* Chicago: University of Chicago Press.

TYLER, R. W. (1966) 'New dimensions in curriculum development.' In *Phi Delta Kappa*, September 1966.

U.N.E.S.C.O. (1959) *Education for International Understanding.* Paris.

U.N.E.S.C.O. (1964) *Youth and Peace.* Paris.

WALL, G. I. (1967) 'The concept of vocational education.' In *Proceedings of the Philosophy of Education Society of Great Britain*, Vol. II.

WHITE, A. R. (1967) *The Philosophy of Mind*. New York: Random House.

WHITE, J. (1967) 'Education for obedience.' *New Society*, 14th September, 1967.

WHITE, J. (1972) 'The concept of curriculum evaluation.' In *Journal of Curriculum Studies*, May 1972.

WHITE, P. (1972) 'Socialization and education.' In DEARDEN, R. A., HIRST, P. H., and PETERS, R. S. (eds.) *Education and the Development of Reason*. London: Routledge and Kegan Paul.

WILSON, J. (1965) 'Two types of teaching.' In ARCHAMBAULT, R. D. (ed.) *Philosophical Analysis and Education*. London: Routledge and Kegan Paul.

WILSON, J., WILLIAMS, N., and SUGARMAN, B. (1967) *Introduction to Moral Education*. Harmondsworth: Penguin Books.

WINCH, P. (1958) *The Idea of a Social Science*. London: Routledge and Kegan Paul.

WINCH, P. (1964) 'Understanding a primitive society.' In *American Philosophical Quarterly*, Vol. I. Reprinted in WINCH, P. *Ethics and Action* (see below).

WINCH, P. (1972) 'The universalizability of moral judgements.' In *Monist*, Vol. XLIX. Reprinted in WINCH, P. *Ethics and Action* (see below).

WINCH, P. (1972) *Ethics and Action*. London: Routledge and Kegan Paul.

WISEMAN, S., and PIDGEON, D. (1970) *Curriculum Evaluation*. Slough: National Foundation for Educational Research.

WITTGENSTEIN, L. (1958) *Philosophical Investigations*, 2nd edition. Oxford: Basil Blackwell.

World Studies Bulletin. A quarterly published by World Education Fellow ship, 18 Campden Grove, London W8.

YOUNG, M. F. (ed.) (1971) *Knowledge and Control*. London: Collier-Macmillan.

Appendix

1. Relevant Schools Council Working Papers

No. 2   *Raising the school leaving age: a co-operative programme of research and development* (H.M.S.O., 1965).

This early working paper pointed the way to subsequent developments of Schools Council work. The view of the curriculum put forward in this paper is therefore holistic. It is suggested that it should possess organic unity, and that the organizing principle most likely to provide a sound basis for development is the study of Man and of human society, needs and purposes. (p. 12)

No. 11   *Society and the young school leaver: a humanities programme in preparation for the raising of the school leaving age* (H.M.S.O., 1967).

This was intended as a discussion paper and stimulant. The main question posed was: what is relevant and interesting to the young school leaver? The main answer was: man himself, his immediate environment and his world wide community. The method of approach was to gather examples of 'the best' practice for public discrimination. The size of the question resulted in a sizable variety of examples, and no clear principles for deciding upon 'the best' emerged. 'Needs', 'interests', 'experience' and 'relevance' were key words, but their meanings remained obscure.

No. 12   *The educational implications of social and economic change* (H.M.S.O., 1967).
This collection of papers begins from the premise that education is in part responsible for the quality of a society's life and will. On the whole, however, the contributors stick safely to fairly general principles.

No. 17   *Community Service and the curriculum* (H.M.S.O., 1968).
Social education requires knowledge of the needs and troubles of their community at first hand. Here then are ways of treating service to that community as a normal part of curricular activity.

No. 22   *The middle years of schooling from 8 to 13* (H.M.S.O., 1969).
The introduction of new subjects to the curriculum generally requires wider reorganization. The development of middle-schools has given the opportunity for re-thinking the curriculum. Two changes might be noticed: first, the more integrated approach to the curriculum; secondly, the renewed interest in social studies. Furthermore, the two changes are not disconnected. See contributions 3, 8, 9, 10 and 15.

No. 27   *Cross'd with adversity* (Evans/Methuen Educational, 1970).
This examines the education of the socially disadvantaged children in secondary schools with various recommendations on curriculum, home-school links, and the training of teachers.

No. 25   *General Studies 16–18* (Evans/Methuen Educational, 1969).
General studies here conceived are so general as to include most things including the social services in contemporary Britain and France.

No. 39   *Social Studies 8–13* (Evans/Methuen Educational, 1971).
This is by far the most useful Schools Council document in this area. It starts with a general overview of social studies for the 8–13 age group. This is followed by a valuable 'typology' of courses—which helps to tidy up the content and approaches in this area. There are valuable examples of courses and a preliminary analysis of the practical difficulties and requirements. The conclusion is provisional viz. the need for a curriculum development project. (See below.)

2. Schools Council Projects

'Moral Education 13–16.' 1967–72. Director: Peter McPhail
The project has devised materials and methods to help pupils adopt 'a considerate style of life in which they take others' needs, interests and feelings into account as well as their own'. Materials were published as *Lifeline* by Longman. This clearly is relevant to certain conceptions of social education.

'Moral Education 8–13.' 1972–76. Director: Peter McPhail
The project is carrying out research designed to increase knowledge of how children learn socially and morally, and to discover what part schools can play and are willing to undertake in this area. In both this and the above projects there are interesting (and not closely examined) assumptions about the interconnection of social and moral education.

'Project Technology 11–18 years.' 1967–72. Director: G. B. Harrison
The project aimed to help pupils to understand the role of technology in society as well as the application of scientific knowledge to practical problems. Publications include *Handbooks* and *Briefs* (Heinnmann), *Technology and Man* (Blackie and University of London Press) *CSE Course Material and Review Material* (English Universities Press).

'Humanities Curriculum Project, 14–16+ years.' 1967–72.
Director: Lawrence Stenhouse
The project developed materials and teaching methods appropriate to inquiry-based courses that cross the traditional subject boundaries between English, history, geography, religious studies and social studies. It has concentrated on developing strategies for the teaching of controversial human issues. Handbooks and materials have been published by Heinemann Educational Books on a variety of social issues. The one on Race Relations was never published.

'North West Regional Curriculum Development Project, 13–16+ years.' 1967–72
Director: Dr W. G. A. Rudd
This project coordinated on a regional basis and produced new curricula and materials in a range of subject areas including social education. MacMillan Educational published *Vocation, Consumer Education, Freedom and Responsibility* and *Conservation* as a result of the cooperative work in the social studies area.

Integrated Studies Project, 11–15 years.' 1968–72. Director: David Bolan
The project investigated the meaning and possible methods of integration in the humanities. The teaching method was based on teams of teachers exploring social themes with their pupils. Packs of materials on *Exploration Man*, *Living Together*, and *Communicating with others* were published by Oxford University Press. Because 'integration' remained ambiguous, it was redefined by the participant teachers in their own ways.

'Social Education 11–16 years.' 1968–71. Director: Prof. H. Davies
This project aimed to provide social awareness through identification with the local community, and possible participation in self-determined social projects. The general idea seems interesting, but very little evidence has arisen from the narrowly based project about how to carry it out.

'History, Geography and Social Science 8–13.' 1971–75.
Director: Professor W. A. L. Blyth.
This project followed from the recommendations of Working Paper No. 39. It aimed to formulate objectives, to identify major integrating concepts, and to produce materials drawn from the three subject areas.

'Education for a multi-racial society, 5–18 years.' 1972–76.
Director: Bert Townsend.
Following the mysterious demise of the Humanities Curriculum Project race pack, this project was established to develop materials which will help teachers to encourage in their pupils rational attitudes in race relations. There is a Schools Council pamphlet on *Race Relations and the curriculum* (1972).

3. Other Projects

Man: a course of study (MACOS), 5–13 years.'
The project is published and disseminated in America by Curriculum Development Associates Limited who stipulate that teachers cannot buy materials unless they attend a training course. It is disseminated in this country on behalf of C.D.A. by the Centre for Applied Research in Education at the University of East Anglia. The content of the course, originally suggested by Jerome Bruner in 'Towards a Theory of Instruction', is 'Man'—'his nature as a species, the forces that shaped and continue to shape his humanity.' Three questions recur throughout. What is human about human beings? How did they get that way? How can they be made more so? It is a highly structured course, very expensive to run, and quite thoroughly evaluated. For further information, write to C.A.R.E. University of East Anglia, Norwich.

'Contra Costa Social Studies Programme, 5–11 years.' Director: Hilda Taba
This programme applies Bruner's spiral of concept development and of the development of generalization to social learning. The Teachers Handbook (1967) published by Addison-Wesley sets it all out clearly.